Rese
Made

Learning Centre

Park Road, Uxbridge Middlesex UB8 1NQ
Telephone : **01895 853326**

Research
Made
Real

A guide for students

Mark Walsh

Published in 2001 by:
Nelson Thornes Ltd
Delta Place
27 Bath Road
CHELTENHAM
GL53 7TH
United Kingdom

04 05 / 10 9 8 7 6 5 4 3

A catalogue record for this book is available from the British Library

ISBN 0 7487 5841 0

Illustrations by Steve Ballinger, Clinton Banbury
Page make-up by Florence Production Ltd

Printed and bound in Great Britain by Ashford Colour Press

Contents

D   **Pulling it all together**

Acknowledgements

The author and publishers would like to thank Patrick McNeill, Graham Ford-Williams and Karen Seymour for their valuable comments on the development of this book.

The author and publishers are grateful to Pavilion Publishing for permission to reproduce the extract from *Mental Health Care Journal* (pp. 105–6).

Every effort has been made to contact copyright holders. The publishers apologise to anyone whose rights have been inadvertently overlooked, and will be happy to rectify any errors or omissions.

Introduction

This book has been written for people who are new to research and are faced with the prospect of having to carry out a small-scale research investigation. In particular, the book aims to help students who are taking a social science based course that includes a research methods unit or module. These courses include the AS/A-level Sociology, Psychology and Social Policy and Advanced Vocational Certificate of Education (AVCE) Health and Social Care awards. As well as covering general principles and approaches to research, the aim of the book is to guide readers through the process of actually doing a piece of practical research.

While writing the book I've tried to take into account the situation and pressures that are typically faced by people doing small-scale research projects for the first time. The book assumes that readers will have a limited amount of time and other resources available to them. I'm also assuming that a research study is only part of what readers have to do alongside other work, study and personal life commitments. As such, the book aims to help readers to control and manage their project, so that it doesn't absorb too much time or get out of hand.

The book has been put together in a way that gives guidance, support and ideas in the areas where first-time researchers tend to need them. I've learnt about this during six years of teaching research methods to post-16 students taking health and social care and social science courses. Many of my previous students have really looked forward to doing their research project, while others couldn't imagine anything worse and began with a feeling of dread. Whichever group you're starting off in, experience tells me that you may well switch camps (a few times) as you experience the research process first hand. Research investigation can be a fantastic and thrilling experience, especially at the beginning and the end of a project. When the going gets tough or feels monotonous, and things just aren't going the way you'd like them to (usually somewhere in the middle of the project), remember to keep it all in perspective. Use the book to help you to focus on and overcome the problems that you face.

Knowledge and understanding of research methods is important in many professions and areas of life. Doing your first project will help you to gain an insight into what 'research' can mean, and it will help you to think critically about the strengths and weaknesses of reported research in the future.

The structure of the book

The book is divided into four parts:

Part A – **Getting ready for research**
Part B – **Preparing for your project**
Part C – **Obtaining and working with data**
Part D – **Pulling it all together**

A

B

C

D

The first two parts are designed to give you the basic knowledge and understanding that you'll need to plan your own research investigation. The second two parts of the book focus on the practicalities of collecting and analysing data and then producing a research report. Overall, the structure of the book follows a step-by-step approach, helping you to get from the beginning to the end of a small-scale project.

Getting ready for research provides an introduction to, and explanation of, the purpose of research investigation. We'll also look at what makes research investigation different from some other forms of information-seeking. Later in this part, we'll be taking a closer look at the ideas and assumptions underpinning two key theoretical approaches to research investigation. The choice that you'll make about which approach to adopt will have a big effect on how you develop your research investigation.

Getting ready for research includes an outline and explanation of the *research process*. This is the secret of any first-time researcher's success, so read it carefully! An examiner and tutor who assesses your research report will be more interested in how you've gone about conducting the investigation than they are in what you've found. I'll make this point a number of times in the book. However, despite being told that an earth-shattering discovery is unlikely to emerge from a small-scale project, there are always some first-time researchers who take short cuts or adopt bad practices in an attempt to produce dramatic findings. Don't do this. Understanding and following a research process will keep you from making such a mistake.

Preparing for your project will take you through the various thinking and planning aspects of your research investigation. The importance of thinking and planning before you collect any data can't be over-emphasised. Careful preparation is your chance to develop a strategy for success, and will ultimately make your life easier. One of the lessons of small-scale projects learnt by many first-time researchers is that they should have invested more time and effort in their preparation.

Obtaining and working with data covers issues to do with carrying out the data collection process and then making some sense of the detailed information that you obtain. Actually getting the data that you need is much less difficult than making sense of it. However, without data you haven't got a research project, so we'll look at some of the dos and don'ts that will help you to get what you need.

When you've collected your data, you'll need to analyse it. We'll look at various ways of doing this.

Once you've analysed your data, you've nearly completed your project. All you have to do is write the investigation up.

Pulling it all together outlines how this is done and what readers expect to see when they open a research report. The section on evaluating research reports should give you an insight into how examiners and other readers of your report will make an assessment of what you've achieved. You may also find it helpful to read this section before you write up your own research report, or as guidance if asked to evaluate a research report yourself.

The book is structured to take you from being a complete novice to an informed small-scale researcher. Some readers may work through it section by section, while others may prefer to dip in and out of it as they require information, guidance or reassurance about the decisions that they've taken. Hopefully, the book is flexible enough to meet various needs and will contribute positively to the successful completion of your research investigation.

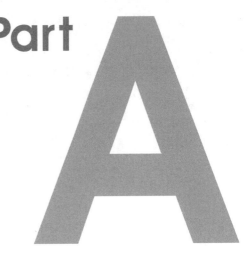

Part A

Getting ready for research

What is a research investigation?

Textbooks usually adopt one of two main approaches to defining what *research* is. The first approach sees *research* as a range of practical skills and activities that are used to conduct particular types of investigation. This approach defines research in terms of what researchers do and the ways in which they do it. A second approach sees *research* as a way of thinking (Kumar, 1996). In this approach, research is about asking critical questions, thinking about and examining evidence and using this to understand phenomena, issues or problems more clearly.

Both of these approaches are useful ways of understanding and defining what's involved in a research investigation. As a result, a third approach is to say that a research investigation involves both a particular way of thinking and an identifiable range of skills and activities. We're going to cover the thinking part in the first half of the book and the skills and activities section in the second half.

Characteristics of research investigations

It's important at this early stage that you see a research investigation as something more than asking a group of people a few questions, or looking up a topic in several books and then summarising your findings. You've probably heard of people doing this and saying that they've done some *research*.

Real research investigations involve more than this kind of general information-seeking. The types of research investigation that we're going to learn about (and which you're going to do) involve:

- Putting forward ideas that can be **tested**

- Collecting **data** to test these ideas in a **systematic** way

- **Analysing** the collected data

- Drawing conclusions based on the research **evidence**

According to Kumar (1996), research investigations should follow a **process** that:

- Is undertaken within a clear philosophical framework

- Uses procedures, methods and techniques that are evaluated for their **validity** and **reliability**

- Is designed to be **unbiased** and **objective**

The term *research process* is very important here. A process is a series of actions or an accepted method of doing something. While research investigation is exciting because it's about discovering and exploring, professional and academic researchers tend to go about their discovering and exploring in a **controlled, rigorous** and **systematic** way. In other words, they follow a **research process**.

Following a research process

A research process is simply a planned, structured approach to inquiry that ensures that your investigation proceeds in a logical, coherent way. There's no one perfect way to conduct a research investigation, so there isn't a single model of the 'research process' as such. There is, however, a broadly accepted series of stages that should be a part of a process of research inquiry.

You'll have to complete a number of different activities as you work through each stage of your research process. The issues and decisions that you'll face as you tackle the activities that are involved in research investigation are outlined in the remaining chapters of the book.

Why bother to do research investigations?

Knowledge produced through research investigation is generally valued more highly than, and can be contrasted with, a *common-sense* or *opinion-based*

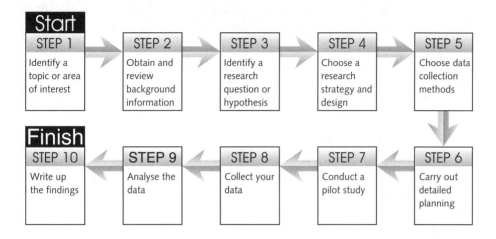

Fig 1   A 10-step version of the research process

understanding of the world. Common sense is based on unquestioned, 'taken for granted' assumptions, while opinions reflect personal prejudices, preferences and ideals. Research-based knowledge, on the other hand, is based on **empirical evidence**; that is, evidence that comes from observation and experience of the real world. There are lots of situations in which common sense and opinions aren't a good enough basis for making decisions or developing understanding. For example, research can provide objective evidence that assists health and social policy-makers in deciding on ways of addressing issues or apparent problems in a local community.

Case study

Meera is a health promotion officer with special responsibility for issues related to sexual health and pregnancy. She is concerned that the teenage pregnancy rate in her town is relatively high compared to other areas around the United Kingdom. The view of many local people is that girls who get pregnant do so deliberately, to gain housing from the council, and that the 'problem' of teenage pregnancy is the result of some girls' bad parenting and poor upbringing. Meera believes that this common-sense, opinion-based explanation of teenage pregnancy is unsatisfactory. She thinks that a sexual health promotion strategy for teenagers should be based on empirical evidence about local teenagers' knowledge and attitudes towards sex, contraception and relationships. Meera's intended research study will look at the sexual health knowledge, attitudes and behaviour of male and female teenagers in her local area. She feels that her research findings will provide an objective basis on which to plan the health promotion strategy.

Researchers generally aim to produce knowledge that's useful and which extends human understanding. The findings of research investigations can, at one extreme, lead to new theories that extend knowledge in disciplines such as health, social care and the social sciences. Other types of research investigations can also produce practically useful findings that influence and help policy-makers and practitioners working in fields such as health, welfare and education.

Types of research investigation _____

When you read or hear people talk about research, you'll come across a number of terms that identify different types of research investigation. The diagram below (see Fig 2) groups types of research under four different headings for simplicity of explanation.

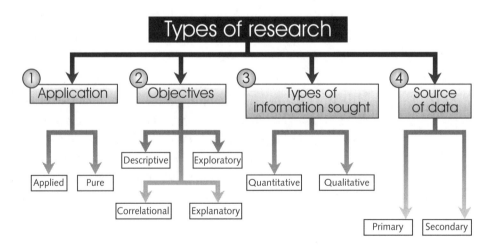

Fig 2   Types of research

Application

One way of understanding research is to consider what the methods used are being applied to – abstract, theoretical ideas or practical issues.

Pure research

Pure research tends to be conceptual rather than practical. It focuses on developing and testing theories and abstract ideas. Pure research may not have any practical application when it's conducted. This doesn't mean that it's any less worthwhile than applied research. It may, in fact, result in theoretical developments that enable other applied research to be carried out at some time in the future, and it can also help to develop an understanding of phenomena, issues or problems at a theoretical level.

Applied research

Applied research is common in the health and social sciences, and is arguably a more appropriate focus for a student research project than pure research. This type of research applies theories and research methods to real situations, problems or issues. The findings of applied research are usually used for a practical purpose, such as making recommendations for new policies, improving practices or procedures or extending understanding of a particular situation.

Objectives

A second way of understanding research is to consider what it seeks to do. Kumar (1996) suggests that research can broadly do one or more of four different things. It can try to:

- Describe something (for example, a situation, problem or practice): this is obviously *descriptive research*

- Establish the links or relationships between two factors (usually called **variables**): this is called *correlational research*

- Explain how and why a link or relationship exists between two factors (those variables again!): this is called *explanatory research*

- Investigate the possibility of undertaking a research study: this is called *exploratory research*

Exploratory pilot research might be conducted into children's interactions in the playground. General observations about what happens during break times (What do children actually do?) could provide the basis for further study. The exploratory study would provide some ideas about what could be researched and what might be interesting.

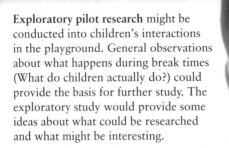

Descriptive research might be conducted to extend knowledge about the different forms of imaginative play in which boys and girls engage at school. Descriptive researchers simply outline (describe) what they observe, answering the question 'What's happening here?' This type of research is often the starting-point for further studies that ask 'why' questions.

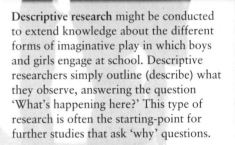

Correlational research might involve a study that investigates whether children use games as a way of making new friends during break times. Correlational research simply establishes whether a link between the two variables – games and making new friends – actually exists. A correlational study could explain *whether* there's a relationship between these two variables, but it wouldn't explain why or how this develops or works.

Explanatory research might involve a study that examines the *why* and *how* questions about the relationships that primary schoolchildren develop in the playground. Research questions such as 'How do children use games to make friends in the playground?' or 'Why are games used to make new friends?' seek explanations. This kind of research is often looking for 'causes'.

Like most research investigations, your own research project will probably involve a combination of the above types of research. For example, you could begin with an exploratory, or **pilot,** study to assess or refine your data collection procedures. You might then collect descriptive data on your chosen subject. This might lead you to extend your study by testing a theory about links between variables in the situation.

The type of information sought

A third way of describing research is to consider the type of data that's being sought.

Quantitative

A **quantitative** study seeks numerical data. Some researchers set out to collect data that measures 'how many', 'how often', 'what percentage or proportion' or 'To what extent is there a connection between X and Y?' When the data has been collected, statistical techniques are used to establish and describe the numerical patterns and relationships that exist in the data. Quantitative research always involves measuring in some way.

Qualitative

Not all data are reducible to a numerical form and researchers don't always want to collect measurements of things. For example, a lot of social science research is conducted into people's experiences. This produces non-numerical **qualitative data.** Researchers who use a naturalistic approach to investigate people's feelings and beliefs, or ways of life, find qualitative data in a variety of sources and are interested in appreciating the 'meanings' attached to them. Research investigations that are primarily seeking these non-numerical forms of data are often called **qualitative studies** (see pp. 89–90 for further details on qualitative data).

The source of the data

A fourth – and our final – way of classifying a research investigation is to identify the main source of the data. The term '**data**' simply refers to the items of information that are produced through research. For example, when using a questionnaire, the 'data' that a researcher collects are the answers that each respondent gives to the questions asked.

Primary sources

Imagine that you actually were asked to carry out research into pre-school children's play. Where could you get data from? One strategy would be to get permission to go to into one or more playgroups or nurseries and observe what happens. The data that you'd actually collect yourself by doing this is known as **primary data**. This kind of data is new, original research information that's directly obtained by the researcher.

Secondary sources

An alternative kind of research information is **secondary data**. It may be appropriate in your research study of pre-school children's play to look at sources of data that already exist on this topic. The playgroups and nurseries may already have some reports or written information about the children's activities. It's also possible that somebody else, perhaps a professional researcher, has already carried out a similar study and produced some useful data. You might also find some statistics on an aspect of young children's abilities or behaviour that you could use in your study. All of these pre-existing sources provide what's known as **secondary data**. The researcher doesn't produce the data personally, but obtains it as a *second-hand* report or record, and then reuses it in his or her own research study.

Case study	Delia studied what young men knew and thought about 'drink driving'. She used a variety of sources of secondary data in her study. Delia began by looking through newspapers for recent stories about drink driving, and obtained some statistics on convictions and road accidents related to drink driving. She also used some psychology and biology books to find out about and make notes on the effects of alcohol on physical coordination and thinking. Delia then carried out three interviews about drinking and driving with male students at her college. She used information from these interviews to identify key sub-topics and issues relating to drink driving. Delia then explored the sub-topics and issues with a sample of male students at her college, using a questionnaire.

There are a variety of ways in which you could use secondary data sources in your own research investigation. For example, you might use secondary sources to find out what has already been researched on the topic that you want to investigate. This would give you 'background' information (see p. 25). Alternatively, when writing up your research report you might compare your own findings with existing (secondary) data on the same topic.

REVIEWING . . .

. . . types of research

What have you learnt about types of research? Check your understanding of the key points by answering the questions below:

– What's the difference between pure and applied research? (p. 5)

– What does descriptive research set out to do? (p. 6)

– What are researchers who conduct correlational research looking for? (p. 6)

– What kind of research asks how and why questions? (p. 6)

– Can you give two examples of secondary data sources that a researcher might use? (p. 8)

– How does primary data differ from secondary data? (p. 8)

– What term would be used to describe numerical information obtained by a researcher? (p. 7)

The answers to these questions can be found on the pages referred to in the brackets that follow each question. If you have difficulty with more than one or two questions, read through the section again to refresh your understanding before moving on.

Theoretical approaches to research _____

The idea of taking a theoretical approach to your research investigation may seem a little bit daunting at first, especially if you see yourself as a practical rather than an academic person. Don't worry – it's not as difficult as it sounds. Basically, you have a choice of two main theoretical approaches for your research investigation. You can adopt either a **positivist approach** or a **naturalistic approach**.

The theoretical approach that you choose will link your ideas and beliefs about 'knowledge' and how it's possible to best understand the world to the practical issue of actually obtaining research data.

The positivist approach

The positivist approach to research investigation is commonly used in the natural sciences (physics, chemistry and biology). It's also widely used by psychology and medical researchers and is sometimes referred to as the **scientific approach**.

Positivist theory is based on a number of key assumptions. It's claimed that:

- Researchers can discover and measure true 'facts' about the world

- Only 'knowledge' gained through *observed experience* is valid and 'scientific'

- Research that's carried out in a controlled and rigorous way enables scientific 'truths' to be discovered

- The researcher can, and should, avoid having any personal influence on the research process

Researchers who accept the basic assumptions of positivism tend to choose data collection methods such as questionnaires, structured interviews and observational checklists, because these allow them to collect 'facts' in a controlled way. These 'facts' tend to be recorded in, or are reducible to, a numerical form. Numerical items of information are often referred to as **quantitative data**.

Positivist researchers typically try to test and observe relationships between 'variables'. Natural or physical **variables** are the characteristics of entities that can be physically manipulated, such as the heat or volume of a substance. For example, the *volume* of alcohol that a person is able to consume before becoming unconscious is a variable that's related, in part, to the person's body mass. Larger, heavier people can generally consume more alcohol than smaller, lighter people because of their greater body mass. Social variables are attributes that are assigned to people and that occur in different levels, strengths or amounts within the population. For example, *marital status* is a social variable that varies in terms of whether a person is single, married or divorced.

Researchers who adopt a positivist approach usually try to **control** the variables that they study. They do this so that they can identify 'cause and effect' relationships between variables. The classic 'controlled' research strategy is the laboratory experiment (see p. 48). Medical researchers, for example, frequently use controlled laboratory experiments to develop, and test the effects of, new medicines. They use this approach to identify the positive and negative effects that their new medicines cause in the controlled experimental situation.

People who put together questionnaires, interviews with pre-arranged questions or observation checklists with pre-defined observation categories are also trying to control the research situation that they're studying. They're also setting limits and boundaries on the possible sources and nature of the data that's collected, by deciding in advance what they will ask about, look for or test.

Researchers who collect data by conducting laboratory experiments impose a high level of control over the research situation, so that they're able to say with certainty how the relationship between the variables works. They're looking for scientific 'truths'. Scientific truths are things that always happen or that apply under specific conditions. A belief in the assumptions of positivism allows researchers to claim that their findings can be **'generalised'**. That is, they believe that their findings are 'true facts' that can be applied from the research setting to the world in general.

Fig 3   Scientific truths are claimed to apply throughout the world, regardless of where they are 'discovered'

Researchers who adopt a positivist approach put great store in maintaining a distance between themselves as 'research experts' and the goings-on in the research setting or situation itself. They adopt the position of very interested, but *outside*, observers of the events that they're studying. Researchers who adopt a positivist approach feel that this is necessary in order to protect their objectivity and avoid influencing, or being influenced by, the people or events that they're studying.

The naturalistic approach

The naturalistic approach to research investigation developed out of criticism of some of the claims and weaknesses of the positivist approach. The naturalistic approach is strongly associated with the disciplines of anthropology and sociology. In care-related research it's likely to be used by members of non-medical disciplines, such as social workers, nurses and occupational therapists, who want to understand the experiences of the individuals and groups that they study.

Naturalistic researchers tend to look in detail at a specific group of people or a particular situation. They don't try to discover scientific 'truths' or establish causal relationships. The naturalistic approach is based on the idea that 'knowledge' is something that people create continuously, and that no fixed, objective reality exists independently of people's culture, values and experience. As a result, researchers using naturalistic approaches don't set out to collect generalisable 'facts'. They try to gain an awareness and appreciation of how particular individuals or groups of people view and experience the world.

Researchers adopting a naturalistic approach base their data collection strategy on the assumption that their main task is to understand reality from the 'inside', from the perspective of the 'researched'. Naturalistic researchers are interested in the *real meaning* of human behaviour and relationships, and believe that this can only be discovered and understood in the **natural setting** where it occurs. As a result, naturalistic researchers tend to use data collection methods such as 'participant observation' and unstructured in-depth interviews, which allow them to gain access to a wide variety of non-numerical **qualitative data**. A researcher adopting a naturalistic approach might be interested in what people say and write, what they do in different situations and how they look and present themselves. All of these data are non-numerical, but if the researcher can appreciate the meaning and significance of the information, it may help him or her to understand what's going on.

Fig 4   Researchers using a naturalistic approach have to be prepared to collect all kinds of data

Most researchers who adopt a naturalistic approach accept that they inevitably play a part in the research situation, and that they should acknowledge this in the way in which they set up, conduct and write up their research investigations. This doesn't mean that the naturalistic approach allows a researcher to deliberately manipulate the participants or bias their findings. It means that they must find ways of identifying and acknowledging how factors such as their existing social characteristics, experiences and culture may affect what it's possible for them to see, understand and experience in the research setting. For example, the existing beliefs and values of the researcher are seen to play an important role in influencing their decisions about what are 'important', 'interesting' and 'useful' data.

Deciding which approach to adopt

While it's possible to distinguish between a positivist and a naturalistic approach to research, you should beware of 'joining a side', as it were, and becoming a positivist or a naturalistic researcher forever! In practice, researchers use both approaches either at different stages in a research investigation (see 'Triangulation – covering all bases', on p. 69) or over a series of studies. Both positivist and naturalistic approaches are useful and necessary for research in the health, social and psychological sciences. Researchers always make judgements about which is the most appropriate approach to use, taking into account the circumstances that they're working in, their subject matter and what they're trying to achieve. This is one of the first tasks that you'll face in planning your research investigation.

Case study

Erik worked in a bookshop café at weekends to earn some money. He gradually developed a fascination with customers' behaviour and decided to explore this for his research project. Erik wasn't sure exactly what he wanted to research, but began to make notes about the interesting and memorable things that happened at work. Over a period of a month, Erik filled a notebook with thoughts and ideas. At first, Erik wasn't sure how he'd use his notes. When he sat down to read through them, he noticed a few themes emerging. He'd been interested in how people who were on their own often managed to keep tables to themselves, how staff tried to avoid getting into conversations with customers and in how parents tried to control their children's behaviour in the café. Erik decided that he'd like to investigate and produce a naturalistic description of the ways in which customers who were on their own used different strategies to create and protect 'personal space' in the café.

How will your research be judged? _____

A first-time researcher should expect readers (particularly coursework assessors!) of their research report to evaluate it in terms of the following criteria:

- The **reliability** of the data collection methods used

- The **validity** of the data that's collected

- The **representativeness** of the research sample or setting used

- The **objectivity** of the researcher

- The **ethical standards** of the research

As a researcher, you'll need to have considered each of these issues at various points when you're planning and carrying out your research investigation. It's important to demonstrate to others that you're both aware of and can provide a considered response to the issues as they affect your research project.

In the next section, we'll look at each of these criteria, except ethics. The ethical aspects of research are covered as a separate topic on pages 70–74.

Reliability

Patrick McNeill (1990) says that 'if a method of collecting evidence is reliable, it means that anybody else using this method, or the same person using it at another time, would come up with the same findings'. As a result, a reader of your research report could have quite a lot of confidence in your findings if your data collection methods were shown to be reliable.

Some data collection methods are seen as being more reliable than others. Data collection methods that involve researchers working on their own, in situations that can't be replicated (repeated) and where the researcher uses his or her beliefs, values or preconceptions to decide which 'data' are important, tend to be less reliable than data collection methods that don't have these characteristics.

Using unreliable data collection methods or tools leads to **validity** problems with the data.

Validity

This concept refers to the issue of whether the data collected is a 'true' picture of what's being studied.

There are many reasons why the data that a researcher collects can be 'invalid'. For example, the data that a researcher collects can be a product of the research instrument that's used rather than a true 'picture', or indicator, of what it actually claims to be. It's relatively straightforward and easy to show that thermometers only measure temperature (heat/cold), but we can be much less certain of the validity of the tools (such as IQ tests) that we use to measure social variables such as 'intelligence'. Do they *really* measure what they claim to measure?

The issue regarding IQ tests is all about their ability and effectiveness to give a true, independent measurement of intelligence. Intelligence tests have been shown to be quite reliable in that if the same IQ test is used on repeated occasions with the same person, they're very likely to produce the same findings each time. This doesn't mean that such tests give valid findings, but just that they're reliable at measuring whatever it is that they're actually measuring. The validity of IQ tests is questioned on the grounds that they really only reveal how good a person is at doing IQ tests – and not the true level of the person's IQ.

Similarly, the validity of the data that you could acquire through using questionnaires and interviews could be challenged on the grounds that your respondents may give you answers that aren't actually true. Such data may lack validity if your respondents deliberately lie, or give answers that don't actually represent how they behave in reality. For example, people who complete questionnaires or take part in research interviews will usually say that they're non-sexist and non-racist, and may well believe this about themselves. While they may not be deliberately lying, their real behaviour – at work and with their friends, for example – may reveal something about their beliefs that they don't wish to acknowledge or admit. For both of the above reasons, the validity of questionnaire and interview data should never be taken for granted or relied upon.

The reliability of data collection methods and the validity of the data that are obtained are always important issues to consider when evaluating your own research or the conclusions that others arrive at when they publish research findings. A third factor that must be taken into account when judging the quality of a research investigation is the representativeness of the data sources.

Representativeness

McNeill (1990) says that **representativeness** 'refers to the question of whether the group or situation being studied are typical of others'. If a group or situation is representative of others, then researchers can **generalise** their findings. That is, they can say that what's true for this group or situation is true of others. If we don't know whether the group or situation is representative, it's not safe, or correct, to claim that the research findings can be generalised outside of the group or situation that has been studied. Researchers who want to generalise their findings use various sampling methods (see pp. 41–46) to try to ensure that their research is based on a representative group of people or a representative situation. There are also many situations in which researchers don't use sampling methods and acknowledge that their findings can't be generalised. For example, researchers who use participant observation (see p. 67) or case study (see p. 52) methods don't usually seek to study a representative group or situation and so don't use sampling techniques.

Representativeness will be a much more important issue for you if you decide to adopt a positivist rather than a naturalistic approach to your research investigation. This doesn't mean that if you decide to adopt a naturalistic approach you'll be able to ignore the issue. People who read your research report will still consider whether your data sources are representative, and will expect to see how you respond to the problems that naturalistic researchers face in this area. At the every least, you'll have to present a justification for not seeking or using a representative sample of people or research setting in your investigation (for examples, see p. 53).

Objectivity

As a researcher you should be objective, as opposed to biased or prejudiced, in the way that you carry out your investigation. As a researcher you must suspend your pre-existing judgements and view the research situation and your research problem from the viewpoint of 'a stranger'. A researcher who is truly objective avoids letting his or her values, beliefs and pre-existing ideas affect or influence the way in which they develop a project, conduct research or analyse the data.

Some researchers, particularly those who adopt a naturalistic approach, feel that it's impossible to be truly objective when conducting research. They argue that a researcher inevitably introduces aspects of their 'self' into the research (see p. 13 for further discussion). The answer to this for naturalistic researchers is to acknowledge their role in, and possible influence on, the research process when they're writing up their account of the research investigation.

In order to be objective, researchers must be open and 'public' in the way that they conduct and explain their research. In your final research report and presentation, it's important to show clearly how you conducted the research, to present your data in an accessible way and to justify any conclusions that you reach. This allows other interested parties to check whether your research has been conducted in an acceptable way, and to evaluate whether the conclusions that you draw are valid and reliable. Objectivity and openness reduce the risk that you'll reach false conclusions, deliberately or accidentally, from conducting a flawed piece of research. In part, objectivity relates to the ethical issue of the researcher being honest. This and other 'ethical' aspects of research investigations are discussed further on pages 70–74.

REVIEWING . . .

. . . how your research will be judged

What have you learnt about how your research will be judged? Check your understanding by answering the questions below:

– Name two things that weaken the reliability of a data collection method. (p. 15)

– What does the concept of **validity** refer to? (pp. 15–16)

– Why can't you assume that interview data is 100% valid? (p. 16)

– Explain why some researchers try to ensure that they select a representative sample of people for their research studies. (pp. 16–17)

– What are you if you're not objective? (p. 17)

The answers to these questions can be found on the pages referred to in the brackets that follow each question. If you have difficulty with more than one or two questions, read through the section again to refresh your understanding before moving on.

Part

Preparing for your project

T he previous part of the book provided you with background information about what a research investigation involves and what's expected of you as a researcher. Bearing this in mind, it's now time to get down to the business of putting your own research investigation together. As I said earlier, you should follow a research process when planning and carrying out your investigation. We're going to return to the 10-step process that was outlined earlier (see p. 3) and work through the various activities that are involved. If you want to get an overview of the whole of the research process, you'll find it presented on page 3.

Identifying a topic or area of interest_____

Starting at the beginning, your first challenge is to identify a topic to research and, within that, a question to address.

This is a creative part of the research process. You'll need to think of some general ideas or topic areas that you're interested in researching. The idea that you end up with will have to be **researchable**. This means that the idea can be **tested** because you're able to obtain **evidence** about it.

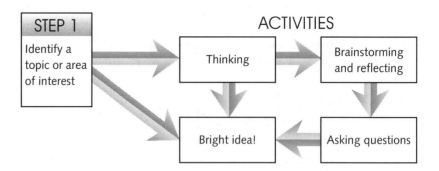

Fig 5   Step 1

Where do research ideas come from?

Basically, you need to have a bright idea. When researchers say that their bright idea 'just came to them', they're not telling you the whole story. Moments of creative insight and inspiration do result in breakthroughs for many people who are trying to think up a good research idea. However, these 'sudden' insights usually occur after the person has done a lot of thinking about different topics without making any apparent progress.

A good way of identifying possible topics to research is to spend some time talking to colleagues about the topics that you enjoy and which interest you. Then think about and sift through the ideas, experiences and interests that you've discussed. This will eventually lead to your moment of insight or breakthrough. You might come up with an idea because you've:

- Studied or learnt about something that was exciting or interesting

- Read or heard about something that you believe isn't true, or which you feel is an injustice

- Discovered a writer, topic or issue that particularly interests you

- Read about a research study that's intriguing, or which you question the validity of

- Always wanted to do a particular type of study, such as participant observation or in-depth interviews

- Met some unusual people, or have access to people who work in settings that are particularly interesting to you

There's no magical or easy way to identify a research idea. Your bright idea is waiting to be identified – you've just got to find it! Remember that it's best to brainstorm and reflect on a range of possibilities before making your decision. Come up with several 'possibles' and then think them over. Peter Langley (1993) suggests that you should ask the following questions about the ideas that you come up with:

- 'Is the proposed research **possible**?' That is, are you likely to be able to obtain primary and secondary data on the subject that you're interested in? Very specialist and sensitive topics may seem glamorous and exciting, but often it's not possible to obtain data on them. 'Pop stars' attitudes to playing live gigs' may be interesting and potentially glamorous, but you probably won't be able to get access to the data that you'd need to make this project work.

- 'Is the idea **relevant** to your course?' The reason for your student research project is to develop and demonstrate your understanding of research skills as they relate to a particular subject area. Your project should, therefore, have strong links to the subject matter of your course. If it doesn't, your work may not be relevant to your course. Could you justify the 'Pop stars' attitudes' idea for your course?

- 'Is the project **interesting** enough to you?' You're probably going to be doing your research project for several months. The topic that you choose should be interesting enough to motivate you to keep the project going until completion.

- 'Is the proposed research **ethically justifiable**?' That is, can you be sure that your research won't cause harm or offence, or get you into difficulties yourself? A project that involves any risk of harm to yourself or others cannot be justified (see p. 70 for further details on research ethics).

Reasons not to choose a topic

There are all sorts of reasons why you might be interested in a particular topic. One of the major problems that first-time researchers encounter is narrowing down the large number of topics that seem really interesting! However, you definitely should avoid some topics – including topics that are so personal to you that they provoke a very strong emotional reaction. You should consider avoiding issues where you have an 'axe to grind' or a very strong moral standpoint. Abortion and euthanasia are examples of topics that have big moral dimensions to them. The reason for avoiding them is that you're likely to bring preconceived ideas and fairly fixed beliefs to the research. These are likely to limit your ability to work through the research process objectively. As we've said, the purpose of small-scale research is more about learning how to follow the research process effectively than making scientific breakthroughs or startling discoveries of particular topics. You must avoid setting out on a project that's simply designed to confirm your preconceptions.

This doesn't mean that you should always avoid a topic simply because you have a standpoint, or have some kind of social, religious or political commitment relating to it. 'Standpoint research' is very common in the field of social policy, for example, and motivates many researchers who wish to make a difference to the aspects of society that they research. People who research poverty, mental distress and homelessness, for example, often declare their personal and professional commitment to helping people who are experiencing these problems. Feminist and anti-racist researchers are also very committed 'standpoint' researchers, and focus on achieving particular social and political goals for women and minority ethnic groups who experience discrimination and disadvantage. However, while professional and academic researchers are expected to use their research experience and training to remain objective, first-time student researchers will find this much more difficult. You'll need to strike a balance between committing yourself to a topic that interests and motivates you and being able to keep an open and objective mind about it.

'Decidophobia' and information overload

When you first try to come up with a research topic, you may experience some confusion and even feel overwhelmed by the task. Many first-time researchers do. It can feel a little like being lost. What you need is a sense of direction.

Finding an initial direction to go in is the key task of the early creative stages of your research project. Some people can't think of any topics at first, while others think of too many possibilities and can't decide between them – this is 'decidophobia'. The possibilities are infinite and this becomes a problem.

If you're finding it difficult to get started, or are becoming overwhelmed, a good 'way in' is to start off by thinking about the big topics that interest and motivate you in your course or area of work. Identify a general subject, or 'big topic', area that you're interested in, such as *health promotion*, *unfair discrimination* or *gender*, for example. Your 'big topic' will be a starting-point – the next step is to refine it.

Fig 6   Choosing a 'big topic' will give your research direction

Activity . . .
. . . Thinking Big

You might like to fill in a copy of the 'Big ideas brainstorm' worksheet (Table 1) to complete this activity.

–   Brainstorm eight different big topics that you might be interested in exploring for your research study.

–   Think about your ideas for a while and decide which topics appeal most to you.

–   Reduce your brainstorm list by repeatedly discarding half of the ideas until you're left with the area that seems the most interesting one to you.

Possible topics	*Second thoughts*	*Semi-finalists*	*The winner!*

Table 1   Big ideas brainstorm

It's impossible to identify a simple list of reasons why professional and academic researchers come up with their research ideas. Some researchers are driven by a personal desire or near obsession to investigate a new topic, or to investigate an established area in a way that nobody else has done before. Only they can explain why. In many other cases, researchers are commissioned, or asked, to conduct investigations by government and commercial organisations. In these circumstances, somebody else comes up with the idea or topic, and the researcher turns it into a research investigation.

Factors influencing the choice of your research topic

- *Values*. A researcher's values can influence his or her choice of research topic and problem. Many sociologists and social policy academics have a strong belief in social justice, and a commitment towards researching and exposing issues such as homelessness, poverty and unfair discrimination, for example.

- *Knowledge gaps*. Many researchers choose their research topic because they believe that a gap exists in knowledge and understanding about it in their particular academic discipline or area of professional practice.

- *Solving problems and influencing policy*. Much social, psychological and healthcare research focuses on solving problems, and is very practical in this sense. Believing that a social, psychological or health problem exists and ought to be dealt with is a significant motivation for some researchers in choosing their research topic.

- *Resources: time and money*. The amount of time and money that a researcher has available places some limitations on what he or she can do. As a first-time, student researcher, you're unlikely to have either much time or much money to lavish on your research investigation. Simple matters such as printing and postage costs need to be taken into account at an early stage. Resource factors can ultimately influence fundamental decisions about the research strategy and methods that are used.

- *Enjoyment and interest*. These two factors should be high on your list of reasons for choosing a topic for your first research investigation. It's important that you choose a topic area that interests you, and that will contribute to the enjoyment that should be part of carrying out a research investigation. If you select a topic that's dull and uninteresting to you, you'll find it hard to motivate yourself and complete the project when you hit a difficult patch, or are under pressure from this and other pieces of work that you have to do.

CONSIDERING . . .

. . . possible research topics

Check your progress so far by working through each of the following questions. Write down your responses to each prompt to demonstrate that you have thought through the various aspects involved in identifying a research topic:

– Have you brainstormed a list of possible research topics?

– Which were the most interesting?

– Have you thought about whether research on the topic is possible, relevant, meaningful and ethically justifiable?

– Can you see any obvious problems in researching the topics that you've identified?

– What factors have influenced your choice of research topic?

If you have other questions, doubts about or problems relating to choosing a research topic, you should talk them through with your tutor or supervisor at an early opportunity.

Obtaining and reviewing background information _____

'Reviewing the field', as it's often called, is an essential task during the planning and preparation stage of your research investigation. What it means is that you'll need to find and review relevant information and previous work done by others on your chosen topic. Professional and academic researchers talk about 'doing a literature review' and spend a lot of their time and energy tracking down and reviewing research literature. In practice, they use specialist, well-equipped academic libraries to identify research papers and books on their chosen topic that have been published throughout the world. Then they review them and

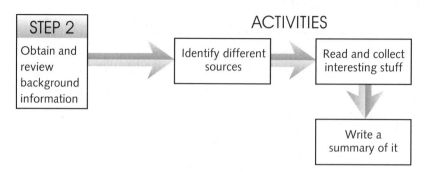

Fig 7   Step 2

summarise the useful bits. However, because you're a first-time researcher, doing a small-scale project and not a Ph.D. (not yet anyway . . .), you should scale down your ambitions. It's unlikely that you'll have access to academic libraries and research journals, so you'll need to concentrate on a broader range of possible background sources. Before we consider what these might be, we need to briefly consider the purpose of searching for and using background information.

Why obtain background information?

There are three main reasons for obtaining and reviewing background information on your research topic.

It will help you to clarify the research problem

In order to obtain background information, you'll need to have a good idea of the kind of things that you're looking for. The process of searching through and reviewing information sources should help you to focus your research idea more clearly.

It will help you to develop your methodology

Finding examples of previous research investigations on the general area – or even the precise problem – that you wish to study will give you a very good idea of how the area can be investigated. Previous studies can help you to develop your own approach, research design and data collection methods. Sometimes it's appropriate to try something different from the work of previous researchers, but there may also be very good reasons for replicating previously used methods. One of the key outcomes of your background information review should be that you'll be able to explain and defend the decisions that you make regarding your investigation.

It should improve your understanding of the research topic

Developing a broader and deeper understanding of the topic area in which you intend to do your research is probably the most important reason for obtaining and reviewing background information. You should know about the theories and evidence that currently exist in your topic area. This will enable you to understand where your own research investigation fits in to the area.

Sources for background information

So, how can you go about searching for background information? The answer to this question will ultimately depend on your ability to gain access to different types of information resources. In theory, a number of potential resources are typically open to public access and therefore suitable for first-time student researchers. These include the following.

Textbooks

You should have access to a wide variety of textbooks in your school, college or local library. Textbooks provide summaries of, and commentaries on, theories and pieces of research, and aim to be as accessible as possible. You may also be able to find examples of statistics, quotes or extracts from important or hard-to-find documents.

A limitation of textbooks as a source of background information is that they provide only **secondary data**. This is in the form of second-hand accounts of research studies or explanations of theories, and is usually fairly brief. Textbooks may be useful in the early stages of your literature search, as you try to get some idea of the kinds of research that have been done on your subject. Use the index of the textbook to identify coverage of your topic within the book, and then make sure that you use the bibliography section to make a note of the reference details. This kind of detail is needed when you come to identify the sources that you've used to complete your project. Reference details can also point you to other specialist topic books, that may or may not be primary sources but which are likely to have more detail on your topic than a textbook can give.

Topic books

A subject or keyword search on the computerised catalogue of your school, college or local library will produce a list of book titles on your topic. These more specialist topic books can be a good source of detail and add depth to your background information. You'll have to work at identifying and summarising the interesting and relevant bits of information that you need. Again, try using the index and reference sections to spot the parts of the book that will be most useful to you.

Journals

Professional and academic researchers publish accounts of their research studies and their findings in specialist research journals. These can be difficult to obtain unless you happen to have access to a higher education library. You may find that some online versions provide full text reports on areas of interest to you.

Magazines

Magazine stories and research findings – particularly in the form of survey findings – may provide you with some useful and accessible background information. You'll need to think carefully about the validity of the information found in magazines, particularly if the magazine is primarily aiming to entertain its readers rather than add anything significant to their knowledge and understanding of a subject. Specialist vocational and subject-focused magazines aimed at professional practitioners and students are likely to be more reliable sources of background information than Sunday supplements or 'glossy' monthly magazines. It's worth looking out for the names of the people who have an established reputation as researchers and authors of books on your area of interest. Many academic researchers write for specialist magazines and are more likely than journalists to make give reliable and valid information on specialist subjects.

Newspapers

Newspapers are often a good source of current information on a subject. The points about reliability and validity of information that were made above also apply to newspapers. The broadsheets (the large-format newspapers) tend to be more reliable and impartial than the tabloid newspapers (those with a smaller page size) as a source of research data and balanced reporting. Again, look out for the names of established researchers and authors on articles that are of interest to you.

CD-ROMs

CD-ROMs are a very popular way of searching for information because they're quick and easy to use. Many of the CD-ROM encyclopaedias do have useful summaries of social science, psychology and health-related topics, but this coverage is always limited. You'll always need further information, and you're unlikely to find up-to-date statistics or accounts of research studies on CD-ROMs.

The Internet

The Internet is very popular with students and other first-time researchers as a potential source of background information for their projects. While it has huge potential and is very convenient as a source of information, you need to be aware that research on the Internet is very different from traditional library research.

The books and journals that you find in libraries have nearly always been through a thorough review and evaluation process by subject experts before they're published. As a result, you can usually rely on the information in books and journals being reliable and objective. By contrast, you cannot rely on websites to be reliable sources of valid and objective information. Anyone can publish anything on the Internet. In some ways this is a strength, but it's also an important weakness for you as a researcher. Because there's usually no review or screening of the information, you'll have to be very careful when doing research online. Here are some useful guidelines:

1   Make use of *both* library and online resources.

2   Cross-check any information obtained from the Internet with authoritative library resources.

3   Evaluate the Internet sites that you use. Ask the following questions:

    - Can you identify the author(s) of the web pages or websites?
    - Are the author(s) well known in the area that you're researching?
    - Do the authors give their credentials and their reasons for publishing the information?
    - Is the site linked to other authoritative and reputable sites?
    - Where did the author(s) gather the information from?
    - Is the information based on original research or secondary sources?
    - When was the information published? (Many sites are never updated or properly maintained.)

- Is the information academic (produced by researchers), popular (produced for the general public), governmental or commercial (produced by a business for commercial reasons)?
- Does the information express an opinion or claim to be factual?
- How does the information compare with what you already know? Does it add anything to your understanding of the topic?

4   Keep a detailed record of the sites that you access and the sources of the information that you use. It's best to bookmark the good sites that you use and organise them in a directory, so that you'll be able to find them again.

5   Reference the sites that you use in your final report.

Organisations

Many commercial, voluntary and statutory organisations conduct research studies that they then publish. If you're able to identify organisations that operate, or have an interest, in the area that you're studying, it's worth contacting them to obtain their publications list. This may reveal the existence of books, booklets, websites and reports that you could use to deepen your under-standing of your research topic. If you're lucky, the information will be free.

The reliability and validity of the information that you obtain is important. It's also important to bear in mind that organisations don't do 'disinterested' research. They usually have a particular set of objectives or goals in mind and do research to further the causes that they believe in. As such, objectivity can be an issue. To assess whether the information that you find is objective, it's best to use a variety of sources and to cross-check between them. This will help you to make judgements about the reliability of each source and the validity of the background information that you collect.

Keeping track of your sources

As a conscientious and enthusiastic researcher, you'll seek out and review numerous pieces of background information from various sources. It's important to keep a record – perhaps using a card index, or a series of record-keeping sheets of A4 paper – of all the sources that you've reviewed and read. If you don't, you'll find that you have to go back and retrace your sources at the end of the project. This can be very time-consuming and frustrating and, with a little advance planning, can be avoided.

Dealing with the information

When you feel that you have obtained sufficient background information, you'll need to summarise it. Basically, you need to write an overview of the main issues, theories and research findings in your area of interest. Do this with your proposed topic in mind. Select the information that appears to be relevant to your topic area. This can take a while to complete, because you'll probably have a large amount of information to deal with. Take your time and try to write a considered, structured summary that outlines the main themes while avoiding too much detail. Your overview should focus the reader's attention on key points and end up by locating your own choice of topic within the overall area. Try to organise your overview in linked, progressive sections such as those suggested by the following statements:

- This is what the topic is about . . .

- This is what people think or have found so far . . .

- These are the main issues . . .

- This is the aspect of the topic that my research is going to address . . .

Your tutor or the awarding body should be able to tell you how long your background information review ought to be. Some awarding bodies give detailed instructions about the length of various components of research reports. You should know the minimum and maximum word counts before you begin, so that you can avoid writing too little – or, more likely, too much.

CONSIDERING ...

. . .background information issues

Check your progress so far by working through each of the following questions. Write down your responses to each prompt to demonstrate that you have thought through the various aspects involved in obtaining and reviewing background information.

- Where can you get your background information from?

- Have you identified a range of different sources?

- What kinds of information are you looking for?

– What are you going to do with the information that you obtain?

– How will you relate the background information to your research idea?

If you have other questions, doubts about or problems relating to identifying and reviewing background information, you should talk them through with your tutor or supervisor at an early opportunity.

Identifying a research question or hypothesis

So, from step 1, you have a 'big topic' to research. This is an important milestone in the life of your project – a breakthrough perhaps, if you've struggled with 'decidophobia'. Congratulations! However, you still need to work on your topic until you know *exactly* what it is that you're researching. You have two things to do. First, you need to focus on a specific aspect of the topic that you've chosen. Second, you'll need to produce a research question and/or an hypothesis. This focusing process is shown in Figure 9.

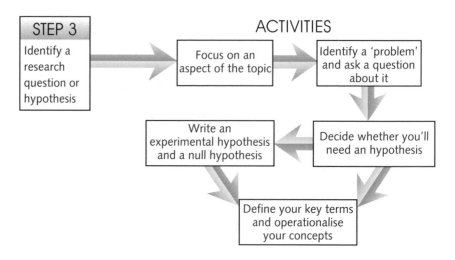

Fig 8   Step 3

Fig 9   Brainstormed ideas have to be worked into a clear hypothesis or research question

Brainstorm – Lots of topic ideas
Choose one big topic – Health risks
Focus on an aspect of this – Smoking during pregnancy
Identify a research question – What do older teenage girls believe are the effects of smoking during pregnancy?
Produce an hypothesis – Teenage girls aged between 16 and 18 attending Iffley College believe that smoking cigarettes during pregnancy causes physical harm to the developing child.

The research question that you choose shouldn't be too wide or too narrow. 'How many Scottish students go to university in England?' is too narrow, because the answer will lack depth and analysis possibilities. Once you've worked out what defines a person as a 'Scottish student', and what counts as 'going to university', the answer will be a simple number. The data won't really say anything about the experience of Scottish students in the English higher education system. On the other hand, 'What's the experience of Scottish students in the UK higher education system?' is too broad and open-ended for a small-scale study. The concept of 'experience' is too vague at the moment and is likely to be problematic. A researchable question lies somewhere between these two examples.

Should you use a research question or hypothesis?

You'll need to produce an hypothesis or a research question to clearly focus your investigation. Your decision about which to use will depend on the type of research that you wish to do and the theoretical approach that you take.

Hypotheses

You may have decided to investigate your chosen topic because you have a 'hunch' about something or you want to test an existing theory. In this case, it would be appropriate to use an **hypothesis**. This is a statement that makes a prediction (your 'hunch') about what you'll find, or what will happen: for example, 'Sociology teachers are more likely to vote for the Labour party than the Conservative party in a general election'. An hypothesis is really a part of a bigger theory about what's believed to be true in the situation that you're investigating. As a researcher, your task is to test the hypothesis (the prediction) by assessing whether the evidence supports or contradicts it. This is sometimes called a **deductive** approach. The researcher tries to deduce, or work out, whether there's evidence to support the hypothesis or 'hunch'. If your research evidence doesn't support the hypothesis (prediction), this might lead you to question and doubt the bigger theory. If the research evidence does support the hypothesis, it might strengthen your belief in the bigger theory. Because the evidence could possibly go either way (supporting *or* contradicting the hypothesis), two hypotheses are needed. Researchers who adopt this approach tend to use what are called an **experimental hypothesis** and a **null hypothesis**.

The **experimental hypothesis** is the predictive statement that you make; for example, 'more water makes tomatoes grow larger'. In an experiment, this hypothesis states that there'll be a measurable difference between two situations that are controlled by the researcher because of the effect of independent variable(s). The independent variable is the factor (amount of water) that the researcher thinks might influence change (growth of tomatoes). However, because the evidence from a research study may not support the experimental hypothesis, researchers produce what's called a **null hypothesis**. This states that any change, or lack of change, that occurs in the experimental situation is due to chance, or to some factor other than the independent variable.

Hypotheses can be **directional** or **non-directional**. If you predict that change will occur in a particular way (for example, that something will increase or decrease), you'll be making a directional hypothesis. If you simply predict that change will occur, without saying how it will occur, you'll be using a non-directional hypothesis.

Research questions

It's not always necessary to use an hypothesis in a research investigation. For example, if you're going to do exploratory or descriptive qualitative research using a naturalistic approach, you may simply want to gain a better understanding of the specific topic that you're investigating. In this case you'd be better off with a research question to guide your work, but you won't need to make any predictions about what you'll find. Researchers who begin with a general question are said to adopt an **inductive approach**; that is, they tend to get very involved in an area and try to work out the sense in the data that they collect. Inductive research works from evidence towards theory – in contrast to deductive research, which begins with the theory and tests it against the evidence.

Research topic	Question or hypothesis	Main methodology
Surrogate pregnancy	Under what circumstances is surrogacy acceptable?	Questionnaire survey
Water birth	What do young women think about water births?	Questionnaire survey and interviews
Informal care	How much support do informal carers feel that they get from professionals?	Questionnaires and interviews
Health promotion	How effective are anti-smoking health promotion materials?	Questionnaires and interviews
Alzheimer's disease	Is it possible to care for people with Alzheimer's disease without using drugs?	Interviews and secondary data review
Cannabis	Should cannabis be legalised for medicinal purposes?	Questionnaires and interviews
Healthcare roles	What are nurses' attitudes towards healthcare support workers?	Questionnaires and interviews
Suicide	Young people under 25 are less likely to disapprove of suicide than people over the age of 50.	In-depth interviews
Gay relationships	Teenagers are more likely to disapprove of gay relationships between members of their own sex than between two members of the opposite sex.	Questionnaires, interviews and a 'photograph response' test
Educational opportunity	Are Asian women less satisfied than Asian men with the higher education opportunities that they have?	Interviews and questionnaire survey
Premature birth and medical treatment	Has the survival rate of premature babies changed over the last 20 years?	Analysis of statistics
Male carers	What do women think of male midwives?	Questionnaires
Children's play	Is there a gender-related pattern to play in the nursery?	Observations and interviews
Smoking	What influences young people to smoke?	Questionnaires and interviews

Table 2   Students' ideas for health and social care research projects

Operationalising concepts and identifying variables

Whatever the research question or hypothesis that you come up with, it's highly
likely that it will contain a number of terms that will need clarifying and
explaining very clearly as part of your project preparation. Look at the following
research question:

- Are Asian women less satisfied than Asian men with the higher education
  opportunities that they have?

You'll notice that 'Asian' (men and women) and 'higher education' are key terms
in the question. These terms need to be defined by the researcher. 'Asian' is being
used to identify a particular type or group of people. But what indicators should
be used to classify a person as 'Asian'? Similarly, what's meant by 'higher
education'? This is a concept (an idea) that describes a particular level of
education, but how should the researcher (and the readers of the research report)
distinguish 'higher' education from other forms of education? Before he or she
can go any further, the researcher has to decide what indicates 'Asian' status and
what 'higher education' includes.

Look at the question again. We still haven't **'operationalised'** the key concept or
idea that we're studying. The concept that we're actually trying to measure is
'satisfaction'. As researchers, we have to decide how to measure 'satisfaction'.
Maybe we could measure it through self-assessed reports of 'satisfaction' given in
response to questioning, or maybe it's the number of applications made to higher
education institutions. Perhaps drop-out rates from university courses are a better
measure of satisfaction with higher education opportunities. There are lots of
potential indicators of 'satisfaction' that could be used, each with their own
strengths and weaknesses. As a researcher, you have to choose the best
indicator(s), the ones that you feel are most useful. When you've clearly defined
all of the terms (we could also call them variables) in your research question or
hypothesis, you'll have operationalised your concepts! In the example that we're
using, this would mean operationalising 'Asian', 'women', 'men', 'satisfaction'
and 'higher education opportunities'. Even though the meanings of some of these
terms seem obvious, it's important to define precisely how they will be used in
your investigation.

The readers of your research report will expect you to explain and justify the
ways in which you operationalise your concepts. When you read research reports
you should also try to find out how the key concepts have been operationalised
and comment on the adequacy of the way in which it's been done.

When you've operationalised your concepts, you'll have a much better idea of your potential data sources, the kinds of data that you're looking for and a clearer idea of the possible ways in which you might go about obtaining it. You'll have said, for example, that an 'Asian' person is someone who identifies his or her ethnic origin as such, and that 'higher' education is indicated by the fact that a person is doing a degree-level course. If 'satisfaction' is indicated by self-assessment of happiness, you'll need to decide how best to collect this data. It would seem that you'd be better off asking questions about this, rather than observing and comparing the body language of male and female students.

Activity . . .
. . . **Identifying and Operationalising Concepts**

Look at the following research question and try to:

1   Define the key terms

2   Identify possible indicators of the key research concept that will help you to operationalise it.

– **Do young women think that water birth is an acceptable way to deliver a baby?**

You might like to write out your own research question or hypothesis, have a go at defining the key terms and then think about how you could operationalise the key research concept.

CONSIDERING . . .
. . . **hypotheses and research questions**

Check your progress so far by working through each of the following questions. Write down your responses to each prompt to demonstrate that you have thought through the various aspects involved in identifying a research question or hypothesis.

– Are you going to use an hypothesis, a research question or both?

– What's your general research question?

- Do you have a null hypothesis as well as an experimental hypothesis, or isn't this necessary?

- Which terms in the research question do you have to define?

- How have you operationalised the concepts that you're going to research?

If you have other questions, doubts about or problems relating to identifying a research question or hypothesis, you should talk them through with your tutor or supervisor at an early opportunity.

Deciding on research design and strategy

So far, you've identified a topic area to carry out your research on, have focused on an aspect of it and have come up with a research question – and perhaps even an hypothesis. The next thing that you need to do is a little detailed, practical planning about how you'll actually approach and structure your investigation. In short, you need to choose a research strategy and decide on a research design. Both of these things must fit your research question and/or hypothesis.

Choosing a research design

A research design is a general plan of how you'll go about running and organising your research investigation. Will you have one data collection period,

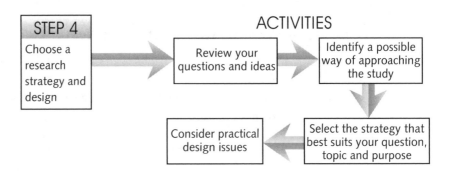

Fig 10   Step 4

or will you collect data before and then after some event (such as an activity or test)? Will you be collecting data about something that's happened in the past (for example, 'how many students cycled to school or college by bike this morning') or do you want to do a comparison of data from two different time periods (for example, 'yesterday compared to last summer')? The various research design options available to you are outlined and discussed later in the book (see pp. 57–62).

Choosing a research strategy

In general terms, a research strategy is an overall methodology. It's a decision about your data collection tactics. For a small-scale piece of project research, the choice is between adopting a survey approach, doing an experiment, carrying out a case study or conducting a piece of action research.

A research strategy is different from a data collection method. Your strategy will define your general approach to the research investigation. The data collection methods that you use aren't predetermined by your choice of research strategy. Whatever strategy you choose, it's generally possible to use a variety of different data collection methods. For example, you could use interviews, questionnaires or observation to obtain data in either a piece of action research or a survey.

Think of a research strategy as a type of holiday. You can probably imagine lots of different types of holiday (beach holidays, skiing holidays and city breaks, for example). Now think of data collection methods as ways of getting to your holiday destination (flying, driving, ferry or walking, for example). You could use most of these methods to go on any type of holiday, but you'd probably choose the most efficient. The same applies to data collection methods. Some methods, such as questionnaires, are ideal for conducting a survey, but you could also survey people's views by conducting interviews, even though it would probably be a less efficient method of collecting similar data.

Your strategic decision about how to carry out your research investigation may be influenced by a number of factors. For example:

– You may want to replicate the methods used in studies and reports that you have read about, where the research topic is similar to your own

– You may want to adopt a particular theoretical approach (for example, naturalistic research) or data collection method (for example, questionnaires)

   –   You'll need to take account of practical factors, such as time and
money. You can't do a large-scale postal survey unless you can afford
the postage charges! You'll also need to take into account the difficulty
of gaining access to important sources of data. An investigation into
the social life of secret agents might prove a bit too difficult for this
reason.

You should make an assessment of the strengths and limitations of the different
strategy options open to you. Do this in relation to your proposed research
project and choose the one that's most appropriate to your project's objectives.
Your choice of research strategy will probably be made at an early stage in the
life of your project.

When choosing your strategy, bear in mind that you won't have that much
time to complete your project. If things don't seem to be working out, it's
unlikely that you'll have the time to start again and adopt a different strategy.
In the next section, we'll consider the various strategy options available to
you.

Surveys _____

Researchers who conduct surveys take a broad, systematic view of a topic at a
specific moment in time and collect empirical data (the observed 'facts') on it.
Survey researchers go for breadth, incorporating data as inclusively as possible,
in an attempt to 'bring things up to date' on their chosen subject.

It's possible to do a survey using questionnaires, interviews or observational
methods, or by reviewing documents. However, most people associate surveys
with questionnaires and interviews as the main data collection tools. The choice
of data collection method tends to depend on how the survey is conducted and
the topic in question. Researchers who use questionnaires and interviews
typically conduct their surveys by post, over the telephone and in face-to-face
personal situations. The advantages and limitations of each of these ways of
conducting a survey are outlined in Table 3.

Survey approach	Advantages	Limitations
Postal questionnaire survey	– Saves on interviewing time – Can reach a large number of people easily – Respondents can think about their answers	– Response rates are often low – You don't know who actually fills in the questionnaire – Can be expensive
Face-to-face interview	– Response rate high – The interviewer can clarify questions – The interviewer can probe replies to get full answers	– Time-consuming – The interviewer may bias or influence the respondents' answers
Telephone survey	– Convenient and quick – The interviewer can clarify questions and probe answers	– Can be expensive – You don't know who is answering – People may not tell the truth, and you can't see their non-verbal behaviour to assess this

Table 3   The advantages and limitations of surveys

The survey population and sampling

If you choose to adopt a survey strategy in your research investigation, you'll need to identify your survey **population** and then select a **sample** from it.

A **population** is the whole class of people or things that you wish to investigate.

Focus of the survey	Who are the population?
Reasons why Oxford United season ticket holders are committed to their team	All people holding an Oxford United season ticket at the time of the survey
The musical tastes of A-level sociology teachers in London	All people who teach A-level sociology in London at the time of the survey
Student attendance records on the last Friday of Christmas term in further education colleges and sixth forms in Birmingham	All attendance registers in further education colleges and sixth forms in Birmingham on the last Friday of the term before Christmas

Table 4   What does a population consist of?

As you can see, the population may – or, in the case of Oxford United, may not – consist of a large number of people or things (such as attendance registers). It's often impossible to distribute a questionnaire to, or conduct interviews with, every member of a research population. Even if you were able to do this, the volume of work – as well as the expense and time – involved in tracking down every population member would probably cause you to give up on the investigation well before you'd finished. The standard way out of these problems is to select a group of people or a number of items out of the whole population, to represent it. This is known as **sampling**.

Choosing a research sample

Ideally, your sample should be representative of the whole population, so that your research conclusions can be generalised (see p. 53 for further details) from it. However, in student research projects the sample doesn't necessarily have to be *precisely* representative of the population. Even so, any lack of representativeness should be acknowledged where it occurs. If you're going to conduct a case study, you don't have to worry quite so much about it being representative.

The first key step in successfully selecting a sample is to ensure that you identify the research population clearly and specifically.

Example
An investigation of the alcohol consumption of . . .

Option 1
. . . AVCE students

Option 2
. . . AVCE students who consume alcohol

Option 3
. . . AVCE students currently at your school or college who consume alcohol

Option 4
. . . female AVCE Health and Social Care students currently at your school or college who consume alcohol

---

In the above example, the population is redefined four times. Each time, the definition becomes more precise. In option 1, the population would be all AVCE students throughout the world. Option 2 narrows this down slightly to AVCE students throughout the world who consume alcohol (there are probably some who don't). It would be impossible to interview or survey a representative sample of either of these large groups. The third option still leaves you with a fairly large group. It would be very difficult to contact and collect data from all individuals who are taking an AVCE course at your school or college, unless you attend a school with a small number of students who are doing AVCE courses. Option 4 is far more realistic, and actually gives you a chance of completing your project!

There should be a list of female AVCE Health and Social Care students who are currently studying at your institution. You could use this list to select a sample. The list of students is known as the **sampling frame**. Professional and academic researchers use a variety of different documents and databases as sampling frames.

Examples of sampling frames

- The telephone directory

- Outpatients clinic lists

- Sports club membership lists

- School/college enrolment lists and class registers

- Lists of employees/payrolls

- The electoral register

- Post Office Address file

- Council Tax Register

In your own research project, you'll need to find an existing sampling frame or, if no sampling frame currently exists for your intended population, you'll have to compile one yourself. Alternatively, you'll have to use a convenience sample or produce some very, very good reasons why you chose another unconventional sampling strategy. There's sometimes a temptation to try to use unorthodox sampling methods in an attempt to take a short cut or give your project something of an exotic edge. Resist it. Examiners are less likely to be impressed by your creative, but flawed, approach to sampling than they are by your clear, conscientious and well-executed use of more standard sampling procedures.

It's best to learn how to use the orthodox approaches before you adapt or depart from them.

The generalisability of your survey findings will depend on whether your sample is representative of the population as a whole. It's important to be aware that the sample will only be representative in terms of particular characteristics. If you want your sample to be representative of the population in a particular way (for age or ethnicity, for example), you'll need to ensure that the proportions in the population as a whole match those in your sample. The sample doesn't have to be representative of the population in other non-targeted ways. For example, it's unlikely that you'd want to ensure an equal height match between the population and sample in a study about sleeping patterns. In that study, height is irrelevant.

When you define your research population, be very specific about the criteria needed for inclusion. As a student researcher you'll also need to ensure that you identify a population to which you can gain access relatively easily. Remember that you'll need to be able to make contact with a number of these people in a relatively short period of time. You'll make the project much more difficult if you choose a population of people who are difficult to identify, track down or get time with.

How big should the sample be?

This is the question that students doing surveys always ask. Professional and academic researchers use relatively complicated statistical techniques to work out how big their samples should be, to make them representative of their research population and to allow them to generalise their findings. In student research projects, size is less important. There are some general considerations to bear in mind, such as the following:

- Smaller samples are less likely to allow you to truly represent the diverse characteristics of the individuals who make up the population (unless the population is also very small!)

- Samples of less than 20 individuals won't usually generate enough data to allow you to produce meaningful statistics

- Larger samples mean that you'll be able to find out less about each individual or case in the sample

Practical considerations, such as how much time you have available, will also affect decisions about sample size. You should discuss this issue with your tutor, who will be able to take into account the circumstances and nature of your investigation. As a very rough guide, a student survey that used a sample of between 30 and 60 individuals would generate enough data for analysis.

Of course, getting 'enough data' also depends on how many questions you ask. If you only ask two questions, you won't have enough data: 15– 20 questions would provide a more adequate and appropriate amount of data. Make sure that you have a mixture of open and closed questions. 'Yes' and 'No' answers don't give much scope for analysis.

Choosing a method of sampling the population

There are basically two approaches to sampling a research population.

Probability methods give each member of the research population an equal chance (or probability) of being chosen as a part of the sample. For example, in our 'alcohol consumption' study (see p. 42) we might select every second female AVCE student from a list provided by your school or college. At the beginning, before we begin to make our selections, every student on the list has a 50% chance of being chosen at random, because we're choosing every second student. Chance will determine which particular members of the sample are selected. The purpose of random sampling is to reduce the potential for bias being introduced by the researcher.

Before you can use a probability sampling method, you'll need to be able to obtain, or produce, a complete list of all of the members of your research population. Remember that this list is known as the 'sampling frame' (see p. 43). The best known probability sampling method is **random sampling**.

One way of selecting members of the population at random is to arrange their names in a numbered list and then use a random-number table to pick numbers from the list. Alternatively, if you have a relatively small number of names you can cut the list up and pick them out at random from a 'hat'. Another alternative is to randomly choose one item to start with, and then to select every name at a given point onwards. For example, you could begin at item six on the list and then select every fourth name.

Random samples can sometimes be non-representative. They can throw up, by chance, collections of people who are somehow not typical of the whole population. The risk of this happening can be overcome by using a second form of probability sampling, known as **stratified random sampling**. This involves identifying subgroups, or strata, within a population and then conducting a random sample of each of these subgroups to ensure that they're all represented in a sample. For example, in our 'alcohol consumption' study it may be appropriate to divide the list up. You could divide it according to age band, whether the person is a first- or second-year student, or even by ethnic group or religious affiliation. Then you'd randomly select individuals from each strata for the sample. This would arguably reduce the risk of obtaining an unrepresentative sample.

In **purposive methods** the chance of a member of the research population being chosen isn't equal and is sometimes unknown. For example, we might select all AVCE Health and Social Care students in the second year of their course at your school or college. In this scenario, the second-year students have a 100% chance of being chosen for the sample, but the first-year students have a 0% chance. Alternatively, we might choose to select all AVCE Health and Social Care students who admit to drinking alcohol. We don't know how many there will be, and so don't know what the chance (probability) is of an individual being selected for the sample.

The best known form of purposive sampling is **quota sampling**. This allows the researcher to control variables in his or her study without having a sampling frame. The researcher must identify the key criteria that all participants need to meet, and then approach people randomly to ask whether they meet these criteria and recruit a 'quota' of this group for research purposes. Once the quota for a particular group has been filled, the researcher won't seek or include any more people from that group.

Quota sampling is useful when the overall proportions of particular groups in the population are known. Quota sampling isn't truly random, as not everyone in a population has an equal chance of being selected. It's a form of sampling that's very useful to students who are carrying out relatively small research investigations in a short period of time. There's no need to have a definitive and complete sampling frame (unlike in stratified random sampling). Student researchers who have a good knowledge of the population that they seek to study can make an informed guess (but should acknowledge this!) to select quotas of individuals who are roughly representative of their research population. In a student research project, the quotas don't need to be in strict proportion to their incidence in the population, but should be roughly so.

The choice of sampling method is usually determined by the need to keep the sampling process as simple as possible, by the likelihood of there being a bias in the sample and by the practicalities of what's actually possible. Choose the one that best suits your project and which you can follow through and complete in the time available to you.

Examples of research using . . .
. . . a survey strategy

Research studies by Mack and Lansley (1985) and Townsend, Corrigan and Kowarzik (1987) illustrate how the survey strategy can be used to conduct research investigations into poverty. Full reference details for the studies can be found at the end of this book. You should be able to locate a detailed account of the studies in sociology textbooks. To find the studies, use the bibliography, index or reference list at the end of the textbook you look in.

CONSIDERING . . .
. . . a survey strategy

Check your progress so far by working through each of the following questions. Write down your responses to each prompt to demonstrate that you have thought through the various aspects involved in using a survey strategy:

- Is a survey the most suitable strategy for your research investigation?

- What data collection methods would you use to carry out your survey?

- How would you conduct the survey: face-to-face, over the phone or by post?

- Who or what will be your population?

- How will you select a sample from within the population?

- Does a sampling frame exist or do you have to create one?

- Will your sample be large and representative enough to generalise from?

If you have other questions, doubts about or problems relating to the use of a survey strategy, you should talk them through with your tutor or supervisor at an early opportunity.

Experiments _____

Experiments are a very common and important research strategy. Like the other research strategies that we've covered so far, there are a variety of ways of collecting data in an experiment. The main characteristics of the experimental strategy relate to *comparison* and *control*, and seeking to find *'cause and effect'* relationships.

Experiments tend to be the strategy of choice where biological, psychological or natural science phenomena are being investigated using a positivist approach. The vast majority of experiments in health-related research are laboratory experiments, or clinical trials, in which the effectiveness of medication and treatments for physical or psychiatric illnesses are investigated.

Social researchers are less likely than natural science researchers to use an experimental strategy. Where they do, they tend to conduct their investigations outside of a laboratory setting and run what are called 'field experiments'. An example might be an investigation into the reaction of members of the public to a person asking directions. In such an experiment, conducted at Paddington railway station, the researcher found that members of the public were more helpful in giving directions to an actor when he was dressed as a businessman compared to when he was dressed as a labourer.

Fig 11   Experiments are controlled situations that allow the researcher to examine 'cause and effect' relationships

Characteristics of experiments

Experiments involve situations in which the researcher identifies two or more 'variables' and then manipulates, or changes, one variable to see what effect, or consequence, this has on the other(s). These 'variables' are called the dependent and independent variables. The **dependent variable** is the thing or behaviour that the researcher wants to explain (such as *anxiety levels*). The **independent variable** is the factor that the researcher thinks might influence the change (such as *large spiders*). The independent variable is the thing that the researcher 'controls' in some way (such as showing people large spiders).

Researchers who use experiments typically wish to generate **quantitative** data and adopt a **positivist approach** to their research investigations. Experimental researchers place a lot of importance on establishing cause and effect relationships and carefully observe and measure what happens in the experimental situation. This is because they don't just want to know whether or not a relationship exists between two variables; they want to find out *exactly how* the relationship works.

Researchers who use experimental strategies make a considerable effort to isolate their experimental variables and reduce the influence of so-called **extraneous variables**. These are factors that may interfere with the relationship between the dependent and independent variables.

In experimental situations, researchers use a number of devices – such as **control groups, placebos,** and **'blind'** and **'double-blind' protocols** – to promote and demonstrate the objectivity of their research. A **control group** is a subgroup of research participants who aren't experimented on. They're usually selected to match the qualities and characteristics of the experimental (tested) group. Findings obtained from the experimental group are then compared to those obtained from the control group (untested).

A '**placebo**' is an inert substance or phenomenon that has no known effect on the variable being tested. For example, instead of being given a real test drug in a clinical trial, some people may be given a placebo, or 'sugar pill'. This looks the same as the real drug, but only contains Vitamin C. In clinical trials of medical drugs it's usual for half of the participants, the 'test' group, to be given the real drug (the independent variable), while the other half, the **control group**, receive the placebo. For the drug to be judged a success, the test group must experience significantly greater change in the **dependent variable** (whatever the intended action of the drug is – for example, mood change) than the placebo group. This would show that the independent variable (the real drug) was the factor that had a significant effect on the dependent variable. In other words, it would show that the drug worked!

Most clinical trials use a **'blind' protocol**. This means that the participants don't know whether they're receiving the real drug or the placebo. Some people who think that they're receiving the real drug but who are actually receiving the placebo will experience what's known as the **'placebo effect'**. That is, they *will* experience some change or improvement – but, of course, this cannot be attributed to the drug!

In a **'double-blind'** study, the participants are allocated to the respective 'test' and 'placebo' groups by an independent researcher, who plays no part in collecting the data about the drug's effects. The researchers who collect and analyse the data don't know which of the participants are in the treatment group and which are receiving the placebo. When the data have been collected and fully analysed, the independent researcher will reveal to the other researchers which participants belong to which group. The aim of all of this is to minimise potential bias and clarify the 'cause and effect' relationship between dependent and independent variables.

Advantages	Limitations
The **reliability** of data collected in experiments tends to be very high, as experiments can be duplicated in exactly the same circumstances.	The researcher can only collect data on a very specific and narrow topic – the relationship between two variables. There's no flexibility beyond this.
'Hard' quantitative data is produced, allowing statistical analysis and comparison between changes in experimental circumstances.	The **validity** of data can be suspect, as the experimenter cannot be certain that he or she has all of the non-experimental variables under control. Additionally, the validity may be questioned because what happens in the laboratory, under controlled conditions, may not happen in the less controlled real world.
The 'scientific' status of the experiment gives it a lot of status and credibility with potential participants.	The use of human beings in experimental situations raises many difficult ethical issues. People have feelings and rights that chemicals don't have!

Table 5   Advantages and limitations of experiments

Example of research using . . .
. . . **an experimental strategy**

Research studies using a field experiment strategy were carried out by Rosenthal and Jacobsen (1968), Mayo (1933), Brown and Gay (1985) and Sissons (1970), amongst many others. You should be able to locate a detailed account of these studies in sociology textbooks. To find the studies, use the bibliography, index or reference list at the end of the textbook.

Psychology textbooks include many examples of classic laboratory-based experimental research. Asch (1956) carried out some famous experiments to test influences on conformity, while Milgram (1963) carried out what are now infamous experiments to test obedience. You'll be able to read a full account of these studies in a psychology textbook.

Full reference details for all of these studies can be found at the end of this book.

CONSIDERING . . .
. . . **an experimental strategy**

Check your progress so far by working through each of the following questions. Write down your responses to each prompt to demonstrate that you have thought through the various aspects involved in using an experimental strategy:

- Is an experiment the most suitable strategy for your research investigation?

- How would you collect the data in your experiment?

- What are your dependent and independent variables?

- How would you control for 'extraneous variables' in the experiment?

- Are you going to use a control group?

- Are there any ethical problems with your proposed experiment?

If you have other questions, doubts about or problems relating to the use of an experimental strategy, you should talk them through with your tutor or supervisor at this point.

Case studies _____

The **case study** strategy involves a systematic investigation into a single individual, event or situation; that is, the researcher studies a single example, or case, of some phenomenon. The chosen case can be a person, group or situation that's researched because of its uniqueness and rarity value. Alternatively, the case might be chosen because it's a typical example of a type of person, group or situation.

Case study research is often conducted over a long period of time, so that detailed, in-depth data can be obtained. Case study researchers value depth more than breadth in their data. A common reason given for doing this is that case studies can 'illuminate the general by looking at the particular'.

Case study research is widely used in the social care and social science field, as it allows researchers to study in detail the relationships of individuals and small groups in their 'natural settings'. For example, when large mental hospitals began to close down in the 1980s, a number of case studies were conducted to find out how the closure process affected relationships between residents and staff. The research findings from these studies gave managers and staff a better insight into the closure process and its impact on various people involved.

Case study research is sometimes described as being 'holistic'. This is because researchers are keen to understand how the various elements and relationships within the case study setting work together. The researcher can then explain *why* certain things happen in the setting, rather than simply stating that they do.

Researchers who conduct case study research make use of a variety of data collection methods, including interviews, questionnaires, observations and analysis of documents. A case study researcher will adopt a 'horses for courses' approach to data collection, and use whatever methods seem most appropriate in the situation. An advantage of this is that data can be validated by triangulation of methods (see p. 69).

If you choose to conduct case study research, it's important that you avoid disturbing the 'natural setting' that you're studying. Case study researchers place a great deal of value on *not* manipulating variables in the case study setting, as they wish to study events and relationships as they naturally occur.

Selecting a case to study

If you decide to use a case study strategy for your research project, you'll have to choose one example of the class of thing(s) that you wish to study. Then you'll need to justify your choice of case! How can you do this? Case study researchers have justified their decisions by saying that their chosen case is:

- A typical example of something, and therefore they've chosen it because this will allow them to generalise their findings to other similar cases

- An extreme example of something, and therefore they can study in depth the particularly unusual quality or factor that makes the case extreme

As well as these justifications, many case study researchers explain their choice of case on pragmatic grounds. For example, a particular case may be chosen because it's more convenient or practical than some other possible case. This is acceptable as long as it isn't the only or main reason for selecting a particular case to study.

The pros and cons of a case study strategy

Using a case study strategy has its advantages and drawbacks for small-scale project research. You'll need to weigh these up in the light of what's required of you, what it is that you'd like to study and achieve, and what you feel about the other strategies that are open to you.

For	*Against*
1 A case study strategy is ideal for collecting data on subtle and complex social situations.	1 The extent to which findings can be generalised beyond the case example that's studied is questionable. Generalisations may not be possible – or, if they are made, they may not be credible.
2 You won't need to try to impose any control over events or variables, as you would if you used an experimental strategy.	2 A case study will generally produce 'soft' qualitative data, which is acceptable if you're seeking a descriptive account, but not so good if you're interested in also obtaining 'hard' factual data that will allow you to make statistical comparisons.
3 Case studies are generally manageable for people who wish to do small-scale project research, because their focus is limited to a defined setting, a group of people or even an individual.	3 You'll have to negotiate access to the case study setting, and ensure that you find ways of limiting the effect of your presence on the 'natural' behaviour and processes of the setting.

Table 6   The case for and against the case study

Examples of research using . . .
. . . a case study strategy

In his study of a secondary school, Ball (1981) provides a good example of a research investigation that uses a case study strategy. You should be able to locate a detailed account of this study in a sociology textbook. Full reference details for the study can be found at the end of this book.

CONSIDERING . . .
. . . a case study strategy

Check your progress so far by working through each of the following questions. Write down your responses to each prompt to demonstrate that you have thought through the various aspects involved in using a case study strategy:

- Is a case study the most suitable strategy for your research investigation?

- How would you select your 'case'?

- How will you justify your selection of a particular case?

- What data collection methods could you use in your case study?

- What would you do to avoid disturbing the natural behaviour of the case study setting?

- Will you be able to generalise your findings beyond the case study setting?

If you have other questions, doubts about or problems relating to the use of a case study strategy, you should talk them through with your tutor or supervisor at this point.

Action research _____

Action research is a relatively new form of research strategy. It has gained a lot of popularity with health and social care practitioners in particular. Action research has become strongly associated with small-scale, problem-solving research that has a practice development goal. In essence, **action research** is a strategy for investigating and solving problems, and a way of introducing and evaluating change. As a strategy, action research provides an opportunity to identify real problems, and then to participate in and evaluate the effects of implementing possible solutions. Action research is really based on a cyclical process that could – in theory at least – never end.

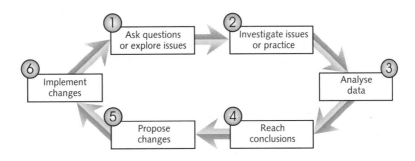

Fig 12   The cyclical process of action research

Action research can be used within both a positivistic and a naturalistic approach to research. As with case study research, the action researcher can use one or more of the data collection methods discussed on pages 62–68. The approach and data collection methods used tend to depend on the disciplinary background of the researcher.

Action research is distinctive in that it encourages participatory research; that is, action researchers encourage the 'researched' to participate in the research investigation as collaborators. In most research designs there's an assumption that the researcher is 'the expert', and that participants won't play an active part in conducting or providing feedback on the research process until it's completed. The participation encouraged by action research results in a shift in power, or 'democratisation', within the research process. This can be seen as positive and ethical, because it gives the 'researched' an important role and 'voice' in the research process. On the other hand, it can lead to problems if leadership of the research process becomes blurred.

When you consider the possibility of using this strategy, bear in mind that action research has to be undertaken as part of some form of practice. To be able to identify and implement 'change' through your research, you'll need to have some kind of 'practitioner' role. It's unlikely that a full-time student would have such a role outside of his or her school or college life.

Advantages	Limitations
1 An action research strategy allows the researcher to look at practical problems and feeds into solutions and changes.	1 Action research is typically small-scale and local to an organisation. This limits the representativeness and the generalisability of any findings.
2 It enables the researcher to develop his or her own practice.	2 'Variables' can't be manipulated, as the research is conducted into ongoing activities and processes.
3 It can provide benefits to participants and organisations.	3 Action research is ethically constrained. It usually affects people's lives' so the researcher must be in a position to take responsibility for all consequences and limit any risks to those affected.
4 There's democratisation of the process through participation by the 'researched'.	4 Within the partnership framework of action research, the ownership and leadership of the research process and findings can be contested.
	5 The researcher needs to be a practitioner in some sense.
	6 Action researchers aren't detached or impartial – therefore it doesn't fit in with 'positivistic' science.

Table 7   The advantages and limitations of action research

CONSIDERING . . .

. . . an action research strategy

Check your progress so far by working through each of the following questions. Write down your responses to each prompt to demonstrate that you have thought through the various aspects involved in using an experimental strategy:

– Is action research the most suitable strategy for your research investigation?

– Do you have a work or other occupational role in which you're a 'practitioner' in some way?

- Do you have a remit to introduce and implement changes in practice in your chosen setting?

- What is it that you'd like to change through your research activity?

- How would you gain the permission of and involve the 'researched' in your investigation?

- Will you be able to generalise your findings from the research setting?

If you have other questions, doubts about or problems relating to the use of an action research strategy, you should talk them through with your tutor or supervisor at this point.

Research designs _____

Where are you now? In terms of progress, you should have:

- Decided on a research topic

- Done a little gathering of background information

- Narrowed your topic down to a specific aspect or research problem

- Produced a research question, and perhaps an hypothesis

- Chosen a research strategy

You've come a long way, but there are still a few more planning activities to do before you can launch into data collection. One of these is to choose a research design. The main purpose of a research design is to plan and explain *how* you'll find answers to your research question(s) and *how* you'll put your research strategy into action. We've got to the point at which you need to think about what you'll actually do in practice in your research investigation. When you're designing your research investigation it's important to ensure that you choose a valid, workable and manageable solution for your particular research project and resources.

Types of research design

There are a number of different ways of defining research designs. Figure 13 divides these into categories according to:

–   The number of contacts that you'll have with your respondents

–   The reference period, or 'time-frame', of the investigation

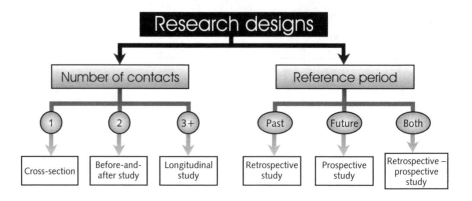

Fig 13   Types of research design

You need to make a decision about each of these issues. How many contacts do you want to have with your respondents? What time-frame will your investigation cover?

The number of data collection contacts

Cross-sectional study design

If you plan to collect data on a single occasion, you'll be doing a cross-sectional study. This gives you a snapshot, or cross-section, 'picture' of the phenomenon and the people whom you're studying, at a particular moment in time.

Cross-sectional studies are the simplest research study designs and are ideal for a student research project (depending on your research question). When you've selected your research problem, you decide what you want to find out, identify the population of people who will be the respondents, select a sample of them (if necessary) and then make one contact with the respondents to obtain your data. An important point to remember is that cross-sectional designs result in a 'still' picture. They can't be used to measure any kind of change.

Before-and-after designs

If, like many researchers, you do want to measure the extent to which change has occurred in some phenomenon, you'll need to select a before-and-after study design. This is also called a pre-test/post-test design, and is often (but not always) used by researchers who are conducting experiments or evaluating the impact of a change in practices or policies. This type of design is really two cross-sectional studies conducted on the same population at different moments in time. Change is measured by comparing the two sets of findings.

By the very nature of having to obtain data at two moments in time, you'll probably have more data collection and analysis work to do than in a single-contact cross-sectional study. This also means that more resources are required, and so a before-and-after study is often financially more expensive to conduct. There are a number of other limitations or weaknesses inherent in before-and-after research designs. These don't always occur, but may do depending on the nature of the study that you wish to conduct:

- **The extraneous variable problem** means, basically, that you can't be sure that the change you're seeking to measure is all caused by the factors that you're studying. 'Extraneous variables' are factors or influences that are outside your control, and are often things that you haven't even considered. The problem is that you don't know to what extent the overall change is caused by extraneous variables.

- **The maturation effect problem** refers to the fact that your respondents may well, especially if they're children or adolescents, change as a result of maturation between the before-and-after data collection times.

- **The reactive effect problem** refers to the situation in which your data collection method (such as a questionnaire or a series of interview questions) actually educates your respondents. This will, in itself, result in some change in their attitudes or behaviour on the topic that you're studying.

Most before-and-after study designs will have an extraneous variable and reactive effect problem. If you do use this type of research design, you should think through the ways in which these problems may have an impact on your findings. They won't necessarily invalidate your findings, but you should indicate that you're aware of the ways in which they may have had an impact on them. More fundamentally, you should consider whether you have enough time available to use a before-and-after design.

Longitudinal study design

A longitudinal study design is used to study a pattern of change over time, or when factual information is required on a continuing basis. Studies of patterns of disease and death rates use longitudinal study designs.

As you've probably worked out, this design involves repeated data collection contacts with respondents. These contacts are usually over a relatively long period. This feature of the design makes a longitudinal study an unlikely choice for a student research project. Despite this, the period of time between data collection contacts isn't fixed and the intervals don't have to be of the same length. For example, in an unorthodox longitudinal study, you could collect data every other day, or two or three times a week. In practice, longitudinal studies usually involve repeated data collection episodes over periods of months or years, not days.

In essence, longitudinal studies are cross-sectional studies repeated a number of times. They're an extension of the before-and-after type of design and, as such, may involve the same weaknesses or limitations. An additional problem of longitudinal study designs is the **conditioning effect**. This occurs where respondents learn what's expected of them, and then either lose interest or behave in a way they think the researcher wants them to. In effect, they have been 'conditioned' by repeated experiences to respond to questions in particular ways, and end up giving their responses without putting any real thought into them.

The reference period

A second factor that affects your research design is the reference period, or time-frame, that you intend to explore. Again, there are three possibilities.

A retrospective study design

This type of study investigates the past. Either it involves either looking at data that has already been collected for the period concerned, or it will be based on what respondents can remember about the situation or problem.

Number of data collection contacts	Type of design	Advantages	Limitations
One contact only	Cross-sectional study	– Simple to plan – Cheap to do – Easy to analyse	– Gives a snapshot only – Can't measure change
Two contacts	Before-and-after study	– Measures change or impact of interventions between two moments in time	– More work than a cross-sectional study – Can be expensive and time-consuming – Respondents can change between before and after points; data then lacks validity – You can't be sure of the effect of extraneous variables on findings – Can have a **reaction effect**
Three or more contacts	Longitudinal study	– Can measure the pattern of change over time	– Involves extensive data collection and analysis – Requires more resources than cross-sectional or before-and-after studies – You need to have a relatively long period of time available to collect data – Data can be affected by the **conditioning effect**

Table 8   The advantages and limitations of research designs

A prospective study design

This type of study design investigates the likely future prevalence of a phenomenon. Researchers using this design consider what the outcome of a situation or event might be.

A retrospective–prospective study design

This type of study design is a hybrid of the previous two. The researcher looks at past trends or data on a phenomenon and then studies what might happen in the future. Before-and-after studies are likely to be retrospective–prospective designs. Part of the data will have been collected before the intervention that's being studied, and then the respondents are studied to find out what effect the intervention has had.

CONSIDERING . . .

. . . research designs

Check your progress so far by working through each of the following questions. Write down your responses to each prompt to demonstrate that you have thought through the various aspects involved in using different research designs:

– What is it that you intend to actually do to obtain research data?

– How many times do you need to obtain data from your participants?

– Do you want to measure change or not?

– How can you minimise the problems that might occur with multi-contact approaches?

– What time-frame will you be covering?

If you have other questions, doubts about or problems relating to a choice of research design, you should talk them through with your tutor or supervisor at this point.

Selecting data collection methods _____

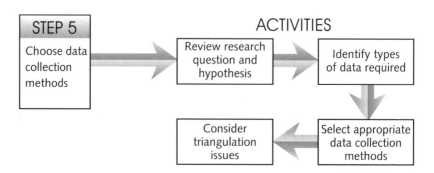

Fig 14   Step 5

We've almost arrived at the part of the process that many people associate with 'doing research' – getting the data. We now need to focus on your main options for obtaining **primary data**. It's important to be open-minded and creative in your selection of methods, so weigh up the strengths and weaknesses of each of the following options before you make your decision.

Questionnaires

Questionnaires are simply lists of pre-written questions and sometimes also include scales. Researchers typically include a variety of **closed questions, rating scales** and '**forced choice**' items in questionnaires. Explanations and examples of each of these can be found in Table 9.

Explanation	*Example*
Closed questions offer limited scope for response. They're usually of the 'yes/no' variety.	Do you smoke cigarettes?
Rating scales require the respondent to indicate a degree of preference or agreement from a limited range of choices.	Choose the item nearest to your own view on the statement that 'Students learn a lot from undertaking work placements.' – Strongly agree – Agree – Neither agree or disagree – Disagree – Strongly disagree
'Forced choice' items set out a possible range of responses, from which respondents then choose. They're generally used to obtain factual information.	Which of the following age groups do you currently belong to? – 14–16 – 17–19 – 20–22 – 23 and over

Table 9   Explanations and examples of closed questions, rating scales and 'forced choice' items in questionnaires

These three kinds of questionnaire 'response item' allow researchers to collect large amounts of quantitative data that can be analysed statistically. Researchers who are adopting a positivist approach often make use of questionnaires to survey a **representative sample** of the **population** in whom they're interested.

Researchers who adopt a naturalistic approach use questionnaire methods much less frequently. Where they're used in naturalistic research, questionnaires are likely to be less structured and less restrictive in terms of the responses that they permit, or are used for triangulation purposes (see p. 69). Typically, the naturalistic researcher would include more **open questions**. These allow for a variety of individual responses and fit better with the aim of getting an 'insider view' of a situation. Open questions also help the researcher to avoid accidentally introducing any of his or her own preconceptions, and protect the validity of the data.

Advantages	Limitations
They can be a cheap and efficient way of collecting data.	It can be difficult to get people to complete. The response rate of postal questionnaires is particularly low.
They can collect a large amount of data relatively quickly.	Respondents often have limited choices of answers. They may not reveal or express their real views or attitudes if they don't match the 'forced choices'. Data collection possibilities are pre-limited by the researcher, as respondents can only provide responses to a restricted range of questions or scales.
They are relatively reliable as a method of data collection.	Unless the questionnaire is conducted face-to-face, the researcher can't be sure of the true identity of the respondent
A comparison of respondents' answers is possible.	The respondents tend to be people who have stronger views or attitudes on the subject being surveyed.
	If the questionnaire is posted, the researcher can't be sure that respondents have understood the questions and can't use follow-up questions to explore unusual answers.

Table 10   The advantages and limitations of questionnaires as a data collection method

CONSIDERING . . .

. . . questionnaires

Check your progress so far by working through each of the following questions. Write down your responses to each prompt to demonstrate that you have thought through the various aspects involved in using questionnaires:

– Why is a questionnaire a good way of getting data for your investigation?

– Are you going to administer the questionnaire face-to-face or by post?

– Will it be a self-completion questionnaire, or will it be completed by you?

– Will you clarify questions or probe the answers that people give?

- How will you identify potential respondents?

- How will you protect the confidentiality of respondents?

- Will you use any rating scales or forced-choice items?

- How will you record responses to open questions?

- How long will it take respondents to work through your questionnaire?

If you have other questions, doubts about or problems relating to the use of questionnaires, you should talk them through with your tutor or supervisor at this point.

Interviews

Interviews are similar to questionnaires in that they're organised around a series of questions and rely on an interviewee being able to answer and tell the 'truth' as they see it. However, interviews are more than long-winded alternatives to questionnaires.

Interviews can be used within either a positivist or a naturalistic research approach, depending on the extent to which they're pre-structured by the researcher. People who adopt a positivist approach will tend to produce a more highly structured schedule of questions that they ask all interviewees. Sometimes researchers who use these **structured interviews** will read out the questions and a limited choice of possible answers to the respondents.

Researchers who adopt a naturalistic approach tend to use **semi-structured** or **unstructured interviews**. In these situations, the researcher has fewer predetermined questions, and is more likely to let the interview develop as a 'guided conversation', according to the interests and wishes of the interviewee. The fact that the researcher is physically present during data-gathering can be both an advantage (people may be more likely to answer questions fully, and the interviewer can ask for further explanation and give clarification) and a disadvantage (their presence may have a 'biasing' effect on responses) of interviews over questionnaires. The advantages and disadvantages of semi-structured interviews are outlined in more detail below.

Advantages	Limitations
It's possible to avoid too much pre-judgement where the questions aren't predetermined. The researcher can obtain the interviewees' 'real' views and beliefs.	The validity of data is always suspect. It's never possible to be 100% sure that an interviewee isn't either deliberately lying or that they can recall the 'truth' correctly.
Semi-structured interviews give the researcher an opportunity to 'probe' what the respondent says. The researcher can also discover and make use of unexpected and unforeseen information as it's revealed.	Recording information can be difficult. Writing down what people say is difficult and can be intrusive. It's hard to keep up, and it interrupts the flow of an interview if you keep stopping to write. Tape recording the interview is much better, but introduces confidentiality issues and may cause the respondent to limit what he or she says.
The depth of information is improved, because the interviewer can explore what the respondent 'really means' or 'really believes', as he or she talks more freely.	People usually give too much information in semi- and unstructured interviews. Most of what they say isn't usable and goes into too much depth.
Response rates can be very good, as the interviewer is present to ensure completion of data collection.	Interviews take a long time to complete, and even longer to transcribe into a written record of what was said.
The researcher can give help and guidance, explaining questions and giving additional information where it's needed.	The reliability of 'data' is poor. It's very difficult to compare responses between respondents, because they may not have been asked exactly the same questions and, as a result, can produce very different data.

Table 11   The advantages and limitations of semi-structured interviews as a data collection method

CONSIDERING . . .

. . . interviews

Check your progress so far by working through each of the following questions. Write down your responses to each prompt to demonstrate that you have thought through the various aspects involved in using interviews to collect data in your project:

– How will you recruit potential interviewees?

– How many interviewees will you need to obtain enough data?

– How structured will your interviews be?

– Where will you carry out your interviews?

– How long will each interview take?

– How will you record what the respondents say?

–   How will you minimise the impact that you, as the interviewer, may have on the participants during interviews?

–   How will you know whether the data that you obtain are reliable?

If you have other questions, doubts about or problems relating to the use of interviews, you should talk them through with your tutor or supervisor at this point.

Participant observation _____

In a **participant observation** study, the researcher enters the group or situation that he or she is studying. Participant observers try to 'get to know' the group or situation from 'the inside'. They need to try to understand the *motives* and *meanings* of the people whom they're studying from the point of view of those people. The aim of this is for the researcher to gain a deeper insight into the real way of life, beliefs and activities of the group in their 'natural setting'. It's believed that the researcher's own experience of the group will give him or her access to data that might not be elicited (drawn out) from a questionnaire or interview.

Participant observation is closely associated with the naturalistic approach to research. It's a data collection method that most positivistic researchers reject, because the 'participant' researcher doesn't remain detached or 'separate' from the research participants or the situation. Because of the danger that participant observation may not produce objective data, researchers often use other methods, such as interviews, alongside it to provide complementary data (see 'Triangulation – covering all bases', on p. 69).

Observational methods can be **overt** – where the researcher identifies him- or herself and their purpose to the people being studied – or **covert** – where the researcher's identity and purpose remain secret. The advantages and limitations of participant observation as a data collection method are outlined in Table 12.

Advantages	Limitations
Observations of 'real' life in natural settings give access to highly valid data.	Researchers may not be able to retain their objectivity or avoid becoming involved in the life of the group. This is sometimes referred to as 'going native'. Researchers may also influence behaviour or events in the research setting if they become too involved.
Observation can produce data that's 'rich' in meaning and may give access to otherwise 'hidden' data.	Participant observers may never really understand the group or setting if they're unable to appreciate the deep meaning and significance of behaviour from the standpoint of a detached outsider.
Participant observers can often obtain detailed data over a long period of time.	Participant observation studies tend to be small scale and the group being studied may also not be representative of any other social group (therefore findings can't be generalised).
Covert participant observation may be the only way of accessing 'hidden' data or hostile groups.	Covert observation has serious ethical implications and problems associated with it. For example, informed consent isn't obtained when covert observation is carried out.
Researchers don't have to decide what they're looking for in advance of beginning their study. They can make decisions about what is and isn't significant behaviour as events occur and unfold naturally.	The **reliability** of observational data collection methods is relatively low, because observations are often personal and non-repeatable.

Table 12   The advantages and limitations of participant observation

CONSIDERING . . .

. . . observational methods

Check your progress so far by working through each of the following questions. Write down your responses to each prompt to demonstrate that you have thought through the various aspects involved in using participant observation methods:

– How will you gain access to the group or situation that you want to observe?

– What can you do to avoid disturbing the natural behaviour of the group?

– Will you make it clear that you're doing research?

– How do you intend to actually record your observations?

– How long will it take to get enough observational data?

–   What will you do to ensure that your observations remain objective?

–   How will you deal with the problem of representativeness?

If you have other questions, doubts about or problems relating to the use of participant observation methods, you should talk them through with your tutor or supervisor at this point.

Triangulation – covering all bases

Professional and academic researchers tend to use '**triangulation**' techniques in their research investigations. Triangulation is a kind of 'belt and braces' or insurance policy approach that's used to try to counter the weaknesses that exist in different methods of data collection and analysis. In essence, when researchers triangulate, they use multiple methods of data collection and analysis.

In the end I decided on three main lines of approach: in-depth interviews, participant observation and a questionnaire. From the interview I hoped to understand the individual as an individual. From the participant observation I hoped to observe the interpersonal level (relationships between members) and from the questionnaire I hoped to see patterns and relationships about which I could only generalise from a large number of respondents.

Source: Barker (1984)

The use of multiple methods of data collection and analysis allows a researcher to benefit from the advantages of each method that they use while trying to minimise the impact of their individual weaknesses. For example, a researcher might decide to use an *unstructured interview* at the beginning of his or her study, to identify what the key issues and terms are, and then use this information to develop a more *structured* set of *interview* questions or a *questionnaire*.

Triangulation-by-method and triangulation-by-analysis enable a researcher to explore various aspects of the same topic, looking at it from different sides or angles. In terms that we've used previously, researchers can collect both **quantitative** and **qualitative** data from **primary** and **secondary** sources. Research investigations that use triangulation tend to be based on one main data collection method that's supplemented by others.

When you're planning your project, you'll need to consider how you're going to obtain data, and what the strengths and weaknesses of your chosen data collection methods are. This is a point at which you should consider triangulation-by-method. If your data collection method has validity weaknesses (interviews) you may want to triangulate with another method in which validity is a strength (participant observation). Similarly, if your method has reliability weaknesses (participant observation) combine it with another in which reliability is a strength (questionnaires).

Thinking about ethics _____

Research investigations are associated with 'progress', 'discovery' and 'improvement' in our understanding of the world. They're generally seen as a good thing. However, in order to be acceptable, any research investigation must be 'ethical'. Research 'ethics' refer to the standards of behaviour and the practical procedures that researchers are expected to follow.

Questions about what is 'moral' (right and wrong) *are* a part of research 'ethics'. However, researchers don't usually have to become involved in deep philosophical thinking about the big 'moral' issues that are a general feature of research. As a researcher, you'll need to find ways of applying a limited set of 'ethical principles' to your own research investigation.

The key criteria that must be met before research is considered 'ethically acceptable' are as follows:

– **Protection of rights**: the participants' right to privacy and confidentiality should be protected

– **Protection from harm**: no harm should be done to others as a result of the research

– **Positive contribution**: some good or benefit should come out of the research investigation; it should result in a positive contribution to knowledge and human understanding

– **Honesty and integrity**: researchers should act in an honest way and be truthful and open in their methods and behaviour

All of your research participants have a basic right to privacy and to be fully informed about what's involved in your research investigation. In order to ensure that you protect the rights of potential participants, you'll need to develop clear, practical ways of gaining their **informed consent** and of protecting the **confidentiality** of the data that you obtain from them.

Obtaining informed consent

As a researcher, you must be able to demonstrate that your research participants have freely given their consent to being involved in your research investigation and that they have a full understanding of what the research involves. They must be aware of the aims of your research and of any risks that they may face if they participate. They must also be fully aware of what they will be required to do or will experience during the research investigation.

How can you obtain informed consent?

First, you'll need to produce a short statement that explains what your study involves. You'll need to either read or show this to each of your potential participants when you try to recruit them as a volunteer. It's an established principle that researchers should not trick people into unwittingly participating in research. **You should not lie to conceal the fact that you're doing research, and all of your participants should be willing volunteers.**

Obtaining informed consent can sometimes be problematic. For example, informed consent is difficult to obtain from children and people with learning disabilities. It's important to remember that some potential recruits are unable to fully understand the nature, requirements and risks involved in a research investigation. It would be wrong to unwittingly involve such people in your research study if you had any doubts about their ability to give informed consent.

You may have read about research studies where the researcher deliberately carried out secret or 'covert' research. These studies usually involve an investigation into a subject that's very sensitive or which involves 'hidden' data. As such, the only way of gaining access to the 'data' was to carry out the study without informing the people being studied. In most circumstances, this is unethical. **You should not carry out a covert study for your student research project.**

Confidentiality

All research participants have a right to privacy. This includes the right to
withdraw from the research investigation at any point if they wish to, the right to
refuse to answer any question asked, and the right to remain anonymous and to
have the confidentiality of their data protected.

In research situations, confidentiality is taken to mean that the information, or
data, given by a participant isn't revealed to others who aren't part of the
research team, except in an anonymous form when the findings of the study are
reported. It also means that the data obtained in the research study should only
be used for the purposes of the research study. No part of it should be sold to, or
be re-used by, people for other research or non-research purposes. Think
carefully about how you'll protect confidentiality if you do a small-scale study in
your local area, school or college. Merely changing participants' names can be
ineffective as a way of protecting confidentiality in such circumstances.

Protection from harm

The golden rule of research is that the researcher should never do any harm to
research participants or those who may be affected by the research. Professional
researchers in health and social care need to clearly identify and document any,
and all, of the risks that participants may face. Research that involved injuring,
maiming or harming another person could never be ethically justifiable. Where a
research study may have a negative impact on the physical or mental health of a
participant, even to the extent of temporarily upsetting them, they should be
fully informed of this risk, and the researcher should take every possible step to
minimise any harm coming to them. **You should not, of course, engage in any
research that may put your participants at physical or psychological risk in
any way.**

Positive contribution

Ideally, a research study should do some good, or at least be of benefit to
participants. Research should not be carried out for the sake of it, or simply to
benefit the career or reputation of the researcher. As a student researcher, you
won't be expected to make a significant contribution to human knowledge and
understanding through your study. It's appreciated that you have to conduct your
research in order to pass your exams. However, you should still undertake your
research with the aim of advancing your own knowledge and understanding, and
you should avoid any kind of frivolous reason.

There are many situations in which research findings aren't as expected, or where they're less than earth-shatteringly important. However, if research begins with a serious and legitimate intention and could potentially have had a beneficial outcome – adding new knowledge to human understanding – it could be said to be ethically justifiable. It isn't ethical if it's frivolous, involves illegal behaviour or unjustifiable suffering, or has no beneficial intention or purpose.

Honesty and integrity

The final ethical principle is linked to the above point, in that it's concerned with the standard of behaviour and integrity of researchers. There's a general expectation that researchers will be truthful and act with integrity. Data must be gathered carefully, findings reported honestly, and any problems, errors or distortions acknowledged. Researchers must never falsify their data or make false claims that aren't backed up by the data that they have. Sadly, researchers don't always live up to the 'ethical' standards and expectations that others have of them. Given the potential implications for people's health and well-being, **a lack of honesty and integrity by researchers is completely ethically unacceptable.**

CONSIDERING . . .

. . . ethical issues

Check your progress so far by working through each of the following questions. Write down your responses to each prompt to demonstrate that you have thought through the various ethical issues involved in conducting your research project:

- How will you obtain informed consent from your research participants?

- What procedures will you use to protect confidentiality?

- How will you explain your confidentiality approach and procedures to potential participants?

- Are there any risks or dangers involved in your proposed investigation?

- How will you ensure that all participants are protected from harm?

- What positive outcomes may result from your investigation?

- How will you demonstrate your honesty and integrity to participants and readers of the research report?

If you have other questions, doubts about or problems relating to the ethics of your project, you should talk them through with your tutor or supervisor at this point.

Detailed planning and the research proposal

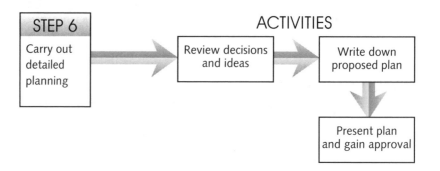

Fig 15   Step 6

Before launching into data collection, professional and academic researchers usually produce a detailed plan of their intended research investigation. This is known as a **research proposal**. Many researchers have to produce one of these in order to obtain formal approval, or permission, to begin collecting data. Sometimes permission has to be sought from the people who are providing the money that will fund the study, or from an ethics committee who control access to potentially vulnerable research participants such as hospital patients. The research proposal outlines what the researcher wishes to do, how he or she intends to go about it and what he or she hopes to gain or achieve through the research investigation.

So far, you've done a lot of thinking and planning. This will have put you in a position to produce your own research proposal. It's useful for all researchers – and particularly for first-time researchers – to produce a research proposal even when there's no formal ethics committee or funding organisation involved. Your tutor may also require you to do this, to ensure that you've completed the required planning stages of the research process. Writing down your ideas and proposed plan in a detailed and explicit way will help you to think through, refine and express your research intentions. It's advisable to include a schedule of work and to identify key dates in your plan at this stage. When you come to do this you may realise that you need to rethink or develop certain parts of your intended project. The research proposal also gives other people, such as your tutor and sometimes the awarding body, an opportunity to scrutinise your investigation plans and point out any weaknesses or obvious problems in it before approval to proceed is given.

A proposal can be set out in various ways. You may want to use the form on page 76 to briefly outline your intentions. Alternatively, come up with your own format and write down your ideas in a logical and clearly explained way. It might help you to follow the stages of the research process when doing this.

1 What's the title/topic area of your proposed research project?

2 What's the research question/hypothesis that you intend to investigate?

3 Explain why you've chosen to study this area and put forward this question/hypothesis.

4 Where will you look for/find possible sources of background information on your chosen topic?

5 Who are your 'research population' going to be?

6 How will you identify a sample of people from the research population from whom to obtain data?

7 What different methods could you use to obtain data for your project?

8 How do you actually intend to obtain the data?

9 Why have you selected this/these method(s) rather than the others available to you? Justify your selection.

10 What ethical issues do you need to be aware of in your research?

11 What will you do to ensure that you conduct 'ethically acceptable' research?

12 What problems/difficulties do you anticipate might occur in your research project?

Table 13   A proposal form – answer each of the above questions as fully as possible to describe the project that you propose to carry out

Part C

Obtaining and working with data

Collecting primary data

When you've completed the planning for your project, have written your proposal and have obtained approval to begin your study, you can start to collect data. It's best to begin your data collection by running a pilot study.

Running a pilot study

A **pilot study** is a small trial run of your investigation in which you check out whether the procedures and methods that you intend to use will actually work. You might run a pilot study to test out your questionnaire, your experimental

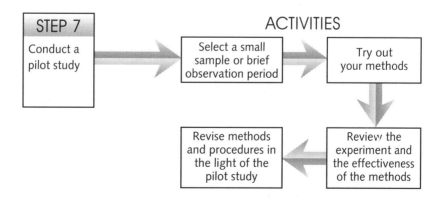

Fig 16   Step 7

procedures or your observational technique. The purpose of the pilot study is to identify any faults or weaknesses in your methods before you try to use them on a larger scale. The pilot study should give you pointers that will help you to avoid problems and improve your intended data collection methods. Many first-time researchers also use a pilot study to gain confidence and develop their basic research technique before embarking on their larger-scale study.

Fig 17   A pilot study is like a test flight

If you want to run a pilot study you'll need to build this in to your time schedule, and also make sure that you don't use up too much of your data source(s) doing it. It's best to discard the data that you obtain in your pilot study rather than include it in any final analysis. Researchers do this because they often adjust their data collection tools as a result of the things that they learn from the pilot study. This will mean that you'll need to find new respondents for your full research project: you should not return to the respondents who took part in the pilot study.

Fig 18   Step 8

Making sense of your data _____

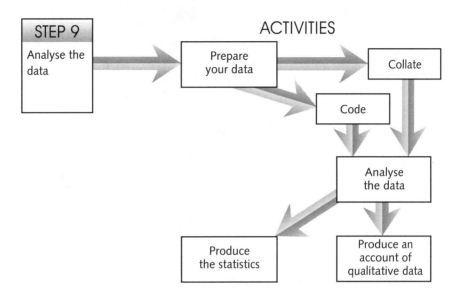

Fig 19   Step 9

Once you've obtained the data that you require, the next task is to make sense of it. This process of making sense of your data is usually referred to as **data analysis**. The way in which you analyse your research data will depend on the form(s) of data that you have. The obvious distinction that occurs is that data can take either a quantitative or qualitative form. It's possible that you'll collect both forms of data in your research study.

Data analysis takes quite a lot of time, so you need to plan for this in advance. First-time researchers often underestimate this and assume that having collected data they've virtually finished their project. Data analysis is an involved and critical stage that still needs to be completed.

Analysing quantitative data

Quantitative data are numerical items of information. When you analyse a set of quantitative data you'll need to use some basic arithmetic, and possibly some simple statistical techniques. Don't be put off by the idea of statistics. In a small-scale research project you'll only need to use basic descriptive statistics in your analysis of the quantitative data. If you understand what the different

Fig 20   Research suggests that 75% of the general public are sceptical about statistics

descriptive statistics tell you about the data, you'll be able to clarify and discuss your findings.

Understanding the data

The process of analysing quantitative data basically involves counting and grouping together answers that are given to each closed question in a questionnaire, and counting and grouping into categories similar types of answers given to open questions. It's also possible to count and group observations that you make using participant observation and content analysis methods of data collection. The extent to which you'll be able to use statistical techniques (even basic ones) on your data and obtain useful information depends on the type of quantitative data with which you're working.

One problem that can occur in first-time research projects is that inexperience leads people to ask questions that produce only nominal data. This means that very little analysis of the data is possible. If you produce lots of nominal data, all you can do is count it up and *report* it. Ideally, you should also be able to compare and contrast, so you'll need to ensure that you collect some ordinal data and, ideally, interval and ratio data if possible.

Type of data	What does it involve?	Analysis possibilities
Nominal data (classificatory scales)	Nominal data are given a number to identify or code them. There's no natural numerical property to the data item, and it isn't possible to measure the 'distance' between data items. For example, characteristics such as a person's sex, ethnicity and place of birth can all be given numerical codes.	You can categorise and then count up the frequencies of each category in the data.
Ordinal data (ranking scales)	These data are assigned numbers to indicate that there's an order or rank between them. For example, strongly agree = 5, agree = 4, no opinion = 3, disagree = 2, strongly disagree = 1. The data aren't naturally numerical.	You can use these data to produce frequencies and simple descriptive statistics.
Interval data	These are recognised measurements, but there's no true zero. The start and end points of the measuring scale are arbitrary. However, the interval between the points on the scale is measurable. For example, temperature recordings provide interval data.	Some basic descriptive statistics can be derived from this data.
Ratio data	These are recognised measurements and have a true zero. Examples include money, age and measures of length and distance. For example, a person who is 20 years old is numerically twice as old as a child who is 10 years old.	You can produce a variety of statistics from this type of data.

Table 14   Analysing quantitative data

Case study

Joanne is doing a research project on the attitudes of AS-level sociology students to women who smoke cigarettes during pregnancy. Her research question is 'Do the attitudes of AS sociology students towards women who smoke cigarettes during pregnancy differ according to gender?' Her hypothesis is that female students are likely to be more critical of women who smoke cigarettes during pregnancy than male sociology students. She has decided to use a questionnaire to collect her data, and has written a number of questions in the hope of obtaining both quantitative and qualitative data.

Joanne asks respondents to indicate:

–   Whether they're smokers or non-smokers

– Whether they strongly agree, agree, neither agree or disagree, disagree or strongly disagree with women smoking cigarettes during pregnancy

– How many cigarettes they themselves smoke each week

Data about whether a person is a smoker or non-smoker is **nominal data**. Answers have to be 'coded' to become numerical. **Coding** simply means creating numbered categories for responses and grouping similar responses together. Smoker may be coded '1' and non-smoker '2', for example. Joanne could then count up all of the 1's (or use a computer spreadsheet and get the analysis done automatically) and work out a very simple frequency distribution. This would tell her how many of the sample are smokers and how many are non-smokers. The only other thing that could be done with this data is to work out the percentage of respondents who fall into each category. You'll probably see that this provides very little in the way of interesting data. The same applies to all 'category' data (ethnicity, gender, age, religious affiliation and occupation, for example) that you collect. Be careful of putting all your quantitative eggs into the nominal basket!

Joanne's question on the extent to which respondents agree or disagree with women smoking during pregnancy offers more analysis possibilities. This is because it produces **ordinal data**. Again, the categories have to be coded to turn them into numerical items of information (strongly agree = 1, for example) but it's possible to make comparison between the categories. For example, she could compare the extent to which male and female AS sociology students agreed or disagreed with women smoking during pregnancy. She might even want to work out some percentages to describe the patterns in her data. If 80% of male students were to disagree with women smoking during pregnancy compared to only 20% of female AS sociology students, Joanne might have the basis for an interesting discussion. What she couldn't say at this point is that gender is the primary influence on AS sociology students' attitudes to women who smoke during pregnancy. Joanne doesn't have the data to support this assertion.

In response to a question about how many cigarettes they smoke each week, respondents would give Joanne an actual numerical answer (for example, 'five cigarettes a week'). This is **ratio data**. There's a true zero figure and the numbers given can be organised into genuine ranked categories (0–5, 6–10 and so on). This true numerical data opens up lots of possibilities for statistical analysis.

Preparing your quantitative data

The first stage of quantitative data analysis involves actually preparing the data to get it into an 'analysable' form. The two things that you have to do with your quantitative data are:

1   Code the responses or observation categories

2   Collate them into a table of responses.

The main method of collecting quantitative data in student research is usually through the use of questionnaires. Most student questionnaires feature a mixture of 'open' and 'closed' questions. Closed questions generally produce quantitative data and are relatively easy to code. We'll look at coding the findings from 'open' questions in the section on analysing the qualitative data below.

Imagine that you're conducting a survey on older teenagers' attitudes to personal relationships and that you're using a questionnaire to collect data on aspects of this topic. Your first two questions require some basic demographic information, while the third and fourth questions seek data on 'attraction':

Example
Attitudes to personal relationships

Question	Code	Type of data
1 What sex are you?		
Male	(1)	Nominal data
Female	(2)	
2 How old are you (years only)?		
15	(1)	Ratio data
16	(2)	
17	(3)	
18	(4)	
19	(5)	

3 Choose ONE response that most clearly matches
your view of the statement below:
'Personality is more important than physical appearance in attracting a boyfriend or girlfriend.'

I strongly agree   (1)   Ordinal data
I agree   (2)
I neither agree or disagree   (3)
I disagree   (4)
I strongly disagree   (5)

4 Describe the characteristics of your own **ideal** partner:

You'll note that the first three questions are 'coded'; that is, the potential answers have all been given a code number in advance. When the researcher has collected all of the data that he or she needs, the next step is to produce a table of coded responses (see Table 15).

	Question 1	2	3
Person A	1	1	2
Person B	2	4	1
Person C	2	4	1
Person D	1	3	3
Person E	2	2	1

Table 15   An example of answers given by five respondents to the first three questions in the above box

You should code all of the 'closed questions' and fixed response items in your questionnaire in advance of collecting any data. You can then just circle the response code that matches your respondent's answer as you work through, asking the questions. When you've collected all of your data, simply enter the response codes into a coding sheet such as this one. Ideally, do this on a computer spreadsheet (or transfer your data to one) as the program will calculate a variety of simple statistics for you.

Making sense of your quantitative data

'**Analysis**' means separating something that's 'whole' into its component parts so that it can be studied. In your case, you'll need to separate a 'whole' data set into its component parts in order to find meaningful patterns and relationships in the mass of data that you've accumulated. Once you've prepared your data, you can analyse it by applying a number of simple descriptive statistics techniques. The basic techniques that we'll look at are:

- Frequency distributions

- Mean, median and mode

- Standard deviations

These are all forms of *descriptive statistics*. They provide a summary of the pattern of information that can be found in a sample. These statistics don't say anything about whether the patterns in your data are likely to apply in, or can be generalised to, the population as a whole.

How to produce a frequency distribution

A **frequency distribution** is a simple tally of how often (or frequently) certain data items occur within a data set. Frequency distributions are used to give simple descriptive information about the variables in your data. To produce a frequency distribution, simply total up the number of each type of response given to a particular question or the number of each type of observation you make. You can then use these numbers to produce a frequency table (see the table in the example below), a bar chart (see Fig 21) *or* a 'pie' chart (see Fig 22).

Example
'Teachers should be paid higher salaries'

A frequency table:

	Code	Number	%
Strongly agree	1	12	35
Agree	2	8	23.5
Neutral	3	5	15
Disagree	4	8	23.5
Strongly disagree	5	1	3
Total		34	100

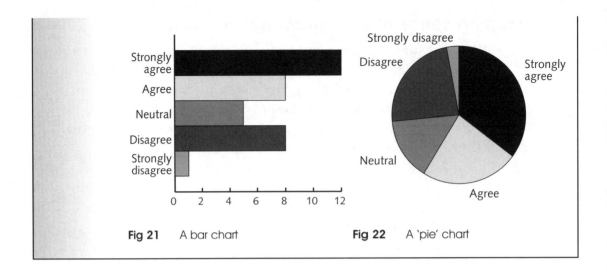

Fig 21   A bar chart   **Fig 22**   A 'pie' chart

Calculating the mean, median and mode

The **mean, median** and **mode** are measures of 'central tendency'. The '**mean**' is the numerical value around which the data is centred. Researchers calculate means in their data sets to get an idea of 'average' values. The mean is easy to calculate (see the accompanying box). You might collect data items that aren't numerical but still want to know what the most common or midpoint items are. The **mode** is the most frequently occurring data item. The **median** is the midpoint in a data set. The example box illustrates these three simple, descriptive forms of central tendency.

Example

Pieces of fruit reportedly eaten by a group of 20 students over a two-day period:

0, 0, 1, 1, 1, 2, 3, 3, 4, 5, 5, 6, 7, 7, 8, 8, 8, 9, 9, 25

Mean = 6

Median = 5

Mode = 8

Calculating the standard deviation

The **mean** shows only where the numerical average is within a data distribution. The **standard deviation** is a measure that shows how much the data varies from the mean. Knowing how much dispersion or spread there is around the mean can be helpful in assessing the extent to which your respondents are similar or different. For example, if most respondents said that they strongly agreed that teachers' wages should be higher, you'd get a low standard deviation and be aware from this that they generally felt much the same. To calculate the standard deviation you need to:

1   Calculate the mean of the data set.

2   Calculate the difference, or 'deviation', between each individual response and the mean value. If the difference is higher it will produce a plus (positive) figure, and if it's lower it will produce a minus (negative) figure.

3   Calculate the square of each of these 'deviations'.

4   Add the squared figures together to get a 'sum of squares' figure.

5   Divide the sum of squares by the number of data items to get a 'variance' figure.

6   Calculate the square root ($\sqrt{\ }$) of the variance figure to obtain the standard deviation.

Example

Let's work out the standard deviation of the data set collected from our fruit-eating students.

Step 1 – the mean of the data set is 6

Step Item	2 Deviation	3 Square of deviation
0	– 6	36
0	– 6	36
1	– 5	25
1	– 5	25
1	– 5	25

2	− 4	16
3	− 3	9
3	− 3	9
4	− 2	4
5	− 1	1
5	− 1	1
6	0	0
7	+1	1
7	+1	1
8	+2	4
8	+2	4
8	+2	4
9	+3	9
9	+3	9
25	+19	361

Step 4 – sum = 580

Step 5 – variance (sum of squares ÷ number of items) = 580 ÷ 20 = 29

Step 6 – square root of variance = 5.385 = standard deviation

The standard deviation from the mean of 5.385 is relatively low. This suggests that the mean is quite a good representation of the average amount of fruit eaten by the respondents over the two-day period. Please note also that, because of the relatively small number of items in the calculation, the standard deviation in our example is statistically questionable. It's just used here for illustrative purposes.

Analysing qualitative data

Data collection methods such as participant observation and in-depth interviews allow less control over the type and range of information that respondents give than methods such as questionnaires. Responses to 'open' questions and observation of 'natural' behaviour are hard to predict. Words – expressing attitudes and opinions, for example – rather than numbers, are the 'units of analysis' produced by qualitative research methods. Both of these factors can cause problems for researchers when it comes to making sense of the qualitative data that they have obtained.

Preparing qualitative data for analysis

As with quantitative data, the first thing that you need to do with your qualitative data is to prepare it for analysis. The two key steps of coding and collating data are again helpful to follow. The difference when working with qualitative data is that the useful items of information are usually a part of a much larger body of information, most of which isn't useful with regard to your research question.

One of the strategies that researchers use to 'capture' data during interviews is to tape record what the respondent says during conversation. This ensures that the researcher get a verbatim, or word-for-word, account, but it also has implications in that the researcher may have to 'transcribe' the interview ('write out' what was said). Transcribing can be very time-consuming. Some researchers find this valuable, as they learn a lot about their data by doing it, while others conclude that wholesale transcribing of interviews is best avoided. Researchers get around the problem of wholesale transcribing by listening to their tapes repeatedly, and using the 'pause' button to allow them to transcribe the most interesting and useful sections. This is one way of beginning the process of coding data. Remember to assess the data in terms of whether it's relevant to your research question.

If you have interviews on a specific topic with several people, or if you've observed a number of similar situations, it's likely that there'll be patterns, themes and similarities in the data. Your analysis task is to find them. You need to decide on some theme or pattern categories (give them a name) and allocate data items to these. You'll need to read through all of your data and assess the 'meaning' of each answer. This requires a careful and sensitive approach to the data, so that you retain the 'meaning' that the respondents intended to give in their responses.

Not all answers will fit neatly into your categories. As a result, you'll need to make some judgements about how to deal with these items – and should acknowledge this.

Making sense of qualitative data

Analysing qualitative data is usually quite an involved and time-consuming process. This is largely because you first have to organise the data into a manageable format. You may have questionnaires with written answers of various lengths to open questions. Alternatively, you may have tape recorded your respondents' answers to interview questions and have a great deal of tape to listen to. Whatever form the data happens to be in, you'll need to reorganise it.

Let's imagine that your qualitative data consists of written responses to three open questions. How can you analyse it? The first step is to make a copy of the original data. You should always keep your original, full data set to refer back to if you need to. Work with the copy. In this situation it would be best to collect together the responses to each question. You might want to cut the relevant sections out of the copied questionnaires. You then need to read the responses several times, thinking about possible similarities between them that could justify grouping them into distinct categories. It's best to do this several times, learning from the data as you do so. Look for themes and patterns all the time. As you can probably imagine, this does take some time and mental effort.

When you've identified themes and patterns, you need to describe them, and perhaps use direct quotes as examples, in a discussion of your findings. You may also want to try to convert some of the qualitative data into a quantitative form to give you further detail to discuss.

Presenting qualitative data

Quantitative data is usually presented in statistical and graphical formats. It's relatively easy to present because it's numerical. On the other hand, qualitative data isn't so straightforward, and requires a more word-based style of presentation. Qualitative data is usually presented as a written discussion. Researchers tend to make use of short verbatim quotes of what respondents said or wrote. They do this to provide evidence of typical or particularly important responses and statements. These are often used to clarify and illustrate the key themes and patterns in the data. In addition to describing and reporting on key themes that are found within the data, qualitative researchers also tend to comment on what was different between respondents, or what was lacking from the data.

While most qualitative research reports depend on written discussions of findings, it's also possible to make use of other devices, such as images, tape recordings, diagrams and flowcharts. These can be used to provide evidence of, and communicate, the key findings. Whatever method is used, the validity of the data should always be preserved.

CONSIDERING . . .

. . . data analysis

Check your progress so far by working through each of the following questions. Write down your responses to each prompt to demonstrate that you have thought through the various issues relating to the analysis of your research data:

- What kinds of data will you have to analyse?

- When will you code your quantitative data?

- How will you do this?

- Will you produce any descriptive statistics?

- How will you prepare your qualitative data for analysis?

- How will you present your qualitative findings?

If you have other questions, doubts about or problems relating to data analysis, you should talk them through with your tutor or supervisor as soon as you can.

Part D

Pulling it all together

Writing a research report _____

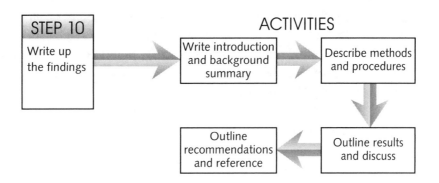

Fig 23 Step 10

Writing up a research report is one of the last stages of completing your research investigation. You're nearly there! Your report should be written in a way that communicates both the *process* (what you did) and the *findings* (what you discovered) to people who read it. The established way of doing this is to follow a commonly used research report structure. Research reports generally follow this common structure because it enables:

- Researchers to outline their research investigation and findings in a logical sequence

- Readers to focus on key features of the research without having to read the whole report

- Other researchers to make comparisons with similar research investigations

- Researchers to guard against writing an account that's biased by their personal views and feelings

Constructing a research report

A standard research report structure is described below, with some guidance on the content of each section.

The title

The title should be informative and should refer closely and descriptively to the focus of your research. The title page should also contain the researcher's name.

The abstract

An abstract is a short summary (100–150 words) of the investigation with 'thumbnail' details, including the aims, methods and main conclusions. Some researchers and awarding bodies refer to this as the **rationale** section of the report. The abstract should be able to stand on its own as a succinct and intelligible summary of the entire report. A clear abstract encourages people to read the entire report. It's often the last task to be completed when writing up the research report.

The introduction

The introduction explains the rationale for the research, summarises background reading about previous work in the same area, and explains the aims, research question(s) and hypothesis (if there is one) of the research. Your goal here is to establish a clear logic, building from a description and analysis of previous research, background information and theory to a statement of the specific purpose of your own research project.

Method

The 'Method' section outlines how you went about the research study. A description of your methods should enable readers to assess the objectivity of your research and whether you adopted appropriate ethical standards. The goal here is to describe your data sources (for example, the sample), the data collection tools that you used and the procedures that you undertook to collect your data. Your explanation should be clear enough for another person to repeat the study in the way that you conducted it.

For ease of reading, divide your 'Method' section into three parts:

- *Data sources*. If people were the key data source, identify the main demographic characteristics of your population (sex, age and so on). If you obtained data from an analysis of texts, TV programmes or some other inanimate source, describe the key characteristics or identifiers of those sources. You should also describe the total sample size, the criteria and method you used to select sample members or items, or the case study situation, and any criteria used to exclude others.

- *The 'Methodology' section*. Identify the method(s) that you used to collect your data. Any questionnaires, observation records or other data collection tools should be described. A full, blank copy of these tools should be included in the appendix at the end of the report.

- *The 'Procedure' section*. This should include a step-by-step account of how you collected the data. You should refer to the conditions under which participants were interviewed or observed, as well as the specific instructions given to them. If you used a questionnaire, you should explain how it was administered.

Findings

The findings of the research should be presented in an appropriate statistical, graphical or written form. You should not include raw data in the main body of the report. At this point, your findings should be described without any further analysis or comment.

'Discussion' and 'Conclusions'

In your 'Discussion' section you should discuss your findings in terms of the patterns, points of interest and conclusions that they lead you to draw. You must be careful to ensure that any conclusions are actually supported by the data that you've obtained. It's a good idea to compare and contrast your findings with those of other similar studies, and with existing theories. You should critically evaluate the validity of your findings and the extent to which they provide answers to the research questions, say whether they support or refute your hypothesis, and comment on the reliability of the data.

Recommendations

You may wish to recommend ways in which your research could be extended or modified to develop or extend knowledge and understanding of the area on which you were focusing.

References

You must reference all of the sources of information that you use in your report. The listing should be alphabetical and should follow a standard referencing system so that the source can be traced (see p. 97).

Appendices

These contain material that is integral to the research, such as a copy of the questionnaire or research/interview notes. While you should keep your original, raw data in case your tutor wishes to see it, it isn't usual practice to include it anywhere in the final research report.

Example
Some dangers to be aware of when writing your final report!

- Don't over-estimate the readers' background knowledge of your topic.

- Don't use long, rambling sentences or explanations. Write simply and clearly.

- Don't use 'I' statements. 'I did this . . . and then I found that . . .' is best avoided. Focus on the topic and the data and write in a non-personal way.

- Don't pad out your report with irrelevant information or pictures.

Don't worry if your hypothesis isn't supported by your findings. You should never falsify your findings or become less objective in your analysis in order to avoid saying that the hypothesis wasn't supported. The important thing is to conduct the research and analysis correctly, so that you can identify when your hypothesis isn't supported by the data! This is perfectly acceptable, and is in no way 'wrong' or incorrect.

Referencing your research _____

One of the final tasks that you'll have to undertake when 'writing up' is to check that you've correctly referenced all of the books, articles and other data sources that you refer to in your report. Remember that you were encouraged to make and keep a complete and accurate record of the sources that you used during your background information search. If you did this, referencing will be straightforward. If not, you can now curse yourself, as you'll have to trace the details of all the sources that you've used before you can move on.

There are a number of standardised referencing techniques that are used by academic and professional researchers. Most journals that publish research reports indicate which referencing system they want authors to use. You just need to choose one and use it correctly and consistently. The **Harvard system** and the **Vancouver system** are referencing methods that are commonly used in research publications. Under the **Harvard system**:

– References are cited in the main text of the report by including the author's surname followed by the year of publication in brackets; for example, Walsh (2000)

– Where there are two authors, include them in the text as, surname and surname (year); for example, Millar and Rogers (2000)

– Where there are more than two authors, insert the first author's surname and then use *et al.* (short for the Latin *et alii*, meaning 'and others'); for example, Johnson *et al.* (2000)

– Direct quotations must be in quotation marks, followed by the author's surname, the year of publication and the page number of the reference (in brackets); for example, 'representativeness refers to the question of whether the group or situation being studied are typical of others' (McNeill, 1990)

– References are listed in alphabetical order at the end of the text, in the same way as on pages 107–108

A journal example using the Harvard system is:

Waring, T. (1996) Prisoners with diabetes: Do they receive appropriate care? *Nursing Times*, **92**(16), 38–39.

A book example using the Harvard system is:

Parkes, C. and Weiss, R. (1983) *Recovery from Bereavement*. Basic Books, New York.

Under the **Vancouver system**:

- References are numbered (number in brackets) consecutively through the text

- Each reference is then listed in numerical order at the end of the text

- Journals are assigned standard abbreviations from *Index Medicus*, the American National Library of Medicine's catalogue of terms and abbreviations

A journal example of a Vancouver reference is:

Waring T. Prisoners with diabetes: Do they receive appropriate care? *Nursing Times* 1996 Apr 17–23; 92(16): 38–39.

A book reference example using the Vancouver system is:

Parkes C, Weiss R. *Recovery from Bereavement*. New York: Basic Books, 1983.

Activity . . .
. . . Using Referencing Systems

Use the Harvard system to correctly reference each of the following:

- An article from Nursing Times (pp. 36–38) called 'Treating obesity in people with learning disabilities', by Michael Perry. August 1996, Volume 92, issue 35.

- A paper entitled 'Pakistani women and maternity care: raising muted voices', written by A. M. Bowes and T. Meehan Domokos, appeared in vol. 18, no. 1, 1996, pages 45–65 of the journal Sociology of Health and Illness.

- An author called Steven Pryjmachuk had a paper published in July 1996 entitled, 'Adolescent schizophrenia: families' information needs'. It was in Mental Health Nursing vol. 16, no. 4.

- A book published in 1996 by Open University Press, Buckingham, by Loraine Blaxter, Christine Hughes and Malcolm Tight, called 'How to Research'.

Example
Tips on writing up

- Follow convention: use a standard report structure in your 'write up'.

- It's easier to write the abstract last (if you're using one).

- Show clearly how your conclusions are supported by the data that you've collected.

- Try to offer some constructive criticism of your own research process and findings. Nobody's research is perfect, and you'll show greater understanding by pointing out the weaknesses and limitations of yours.

- Remember to say whether your findings support or refute the original hypothesis, or how they answer the initial research question.

- Reference your work fully and accurately.

- Check that your spelling and grammar are correct. Word processor programs can help you to do this. However, don't rely totally on spell-checkers. You should still proof-read your work afterwards to cheque for odd errors that the spell-checker overlooks!

- Word processing is a good way of ensuring that your work is neatly presented.

Appendix: Evaluating research reports

Budding social researchers like yourself are often asked, as part of the learning and skills development process, to evaluate other people's research reports. An evaluation involves making a judgement about the relative strengths, weaknesses or overall value of something. When you evaluate a research report, you should look for answers to the following questions:

- What's the research question or hypothesis?

- Why is it said to be interesting or important?

- How was the research investigation carried out?

- What were the key findings?

- How, if at all, do the findings provide a valid answer to the original question or hypothesis?

It might be useful to know that these are the kinds of questions that the examiner, and other readers, of your own research report will be asking themselves. You may want to take this fact into account when writing up your report.

How to evaluate a research report _____

Step 1 – read the report carefully

First, you'll need to find out what the research report actually says. It's best to read the report in a way that enables you to answer the questions that you want to ask (see above), rather than reading it from beginning to end in a conventional manner. Start with the title and the abstract or summary, if the report has one. This will give you an overview of what the paper is about and the kind of conclusions that are reached.

So, you've got an idea of what the report is about. The next thing that you'll want to know is: What was the research question or hypothesis? What question was the researcher trying to answer? Perhaps he or she was trying to explore an issue or demonstrate a link between particular variables. There'll be some unknown area on which the research is trying to cast some light. You need to identify it. You should try to identify the aims and objectives of the investigation. The introductory section usually tells you what these are, but check the background literature review and comments to see if these things are spelt out there.

Now that you know what the questions were, it's time to look for the answers that were found. What does the researcher claim to have found out? Try to identify the answers that are offered for each research question that has been posed. The places to look are in the 'Findings', 'Results', 'Discussion' and/or 'Conclusions' sections.

Step 2 – examine the methods

You know the questions and the answers resulting from the investigation. The next step is to examine the methods used. You need to find out what the researcher did and how he or she did it. In other words, what research strategy, design, data collection and sampling methods were used? You could break this down into a series of further questions and make notes about each:

- Was the strategy a survey, an experiment, a case study or an observation? Under what circumstances were the data collected? What biases might this have introduced?

- Who, or what population, was the study about? How was sampling carried out? How many cases were sampled? Are there any potential sampling biases?

— What data were collected? How was this done? How did the researcher operationalise his or her concepts?

Step 3 – summarise

Your evaluation is likely to need a summary of some sort. Basically, you need to provide a brief descriptive account of what the research was about, how it was done and what was found. Try to be clear, precise and unambiguous in the way in which you report on the study.

Step 4 – be critical

Most evaluations require you to be critical. This isn't an opportunity to say that everything about the study was awful – or an invitation to criticise the researcher in any personal sense. A critical evaluation requires you to identify the relative strengths and weaknesses of the methods used in the study, and to assess the findings and conclusions in the light of the methods used to obtain them. Work your way through the findings and match it up to the conclusions. Check that each of the conclusions is supported by the researcher's findings. You may want to raise doubts about the validity of some findings in the light of the methods used to collect it. You'll then have to decide whether the conclusions still hold, despite the weaknesses that you see in the evidence.

Step 5 – write a critique

A critique is a considered, argued but balanced appraisal of the research report. Approach it in an objective and structured way:

— Begin with a balanced account of the research study.

— Next, identify and discuss the strengths of the researcher's approach.

— Move on to identify any parts of the original questions or objectives that the research doesn't seem to address.

— You might then discuss the logic of the argument(s) that the researcher puts forward, particularly if there are contradictions or problems with them.

— Now you're left with the conclusions. Consider the areas in which the evidence for the conclusions is either strong or weak. You may want to comment on the extent to which the methods used to obtain the data limit the generalisability or validity of the conclusions.

– Towards the end of your critique you'll need to look at ethical issues. Appraise the extent to which the researcher protected or placed participants 'at risk', and assess the adequacy of the confidentiality procedures and the efforts made to avoid introducing bias.

– Finally, you'll need to arrive at a conclusion about the research study that you're appraising. You'll need to identify what has – and what hasn't – been shown to be true, and what you feel the overall strengths and weaknesses of the investigation were.

PAPERS
DRUG ADDICTION

Hallucinogenic drug use among young people in Spain: a comparative study

Natividad Martìnez Diez
DUE

Luis Lopez Rodriguez
DUE

Cristina Casado
Gonzalez DUE

Sonia Gonzalez Delgado
DUE
*Psychiatric department
University of Oviedo
Spain*

Adolescence is a difficult period in life, when young people are vulnerable to an array of pressures which make them more vulnerable to experimentation with drugs, potentially leading to addiction and serious health problems. NATIVIDAD MARTINEZ DIEZ and colleagues describe a study of drug misuse among young people in the city of Oviedo in Spain. Mental Health Care 1999; 2, 10: 346-347

Adolescence is a difficult period for young people, when they go through many psychological, intellectual, moral and emotional changes. The main characteristic of this period is a quest for identity and the struggle to establish a sense of self.[1] This age group is particularly vulnerable to experimentation with hallucinogenic drugs. It may not be their first contact with illegal drugs, but it is one of the most important.

This study centres on the consumption of in particular lysergic acid diethylamide, more commonly known as LSD. LSD is a synthetic drug derived from ergot of rye which acts on the nervous system, leading to visual hallucinations.[2] LSD also acts on the nervous system, producing reactions such as trembling, hypertension, nausea and vomiting. Use of LSD in Spain has been illegal since 1966. The Spanish government subsequently updated the list of prohibited drugs to include other hallucinogenics such as MDMA (ecstasy). This study seeks to identify some of the factors which may make some young people more vulnerable to experimentation and drug addiction, by comparing three distinct social groups: secondary school students, medical and nursing students, and army conscripts.

Method

A sample of 1254 young people – 704 males and 546 females – was identified, in three social groups. Group one comprised 602 students enrolled on health sciences programmes at Oviedo University. These were second, fourth and sixth year medical students, and first, second and third year nursing and physiotherapy students. Of the 602, 159 (27%) were male and 439 (73%) female. The breakdown by studies was 83 (14%) physiotherapy students, 242 (42%) nursing students, and 277 (46%) medical students. Group two comprised 409 young men doing their compulsory military service, based at a barracks in the principality of Asturias, where Oviedo is situated. Group three comprised 243 secondary school students attending the Institute Perez de Ayala: a state school on the outskirts of Oviedo. Of these, 136 (56%) were male and 107 (44%) female. The total sample provided a cross section of population of young people aged 14 upwards in Oviedo: in particular aged 14 to 16.

To carry out the study we wanted a questionnaire about drug use that would be easy to understand and answer, not too long, and familiar to those working in health and drug abuse services. We chose the Questionnaire on Tobacco, Alcohol and Drugs, based on an updated version of the Methodologie pour des enquêtes sur l'usage des drogues chez etudiants, to which we added two variables: sex and age.[3]

The questionnaire comprised 71 questions in all, and was divided into separate sections on smoking, alcohol and drugs. The questionnaires were distributed directly to participants by members of the investigation team, as we were familiar with the contents and could answer any queries arising from it. We felt this would also encourage participants to be more open in their replies than if the questionnaire had been administered by education staff or senior army officers. Only with the conscript group were we not allowed to give out the questionnaire for individuals to complete on their own. The conscripts were assembled in a large hall, and given answer sheets and the questions read out to them. None of the participants was given prior notice of the study. Anonymity was guaranteed, and the fact that participation was voluntary was made clear.

Statistical processing was undertaken at Oviedo University psychiatric department, using DBase 3P software and the SPSS/PC+ data package. The analysis sought to compare the frequency of consumption of hallucinogenic drugs between the three groups.

Results

A total of 1254 completed questionnaires were returned. The results showed that the young people in the conscript group were most likely to have tried drugs at least once (6.9 per cent), and at a younger age than either of the other groups (figure one). Next were the secondary students, 5.8 per cent of whom had used drugs at least once. This was higher than that recorded for secondary school students in Spain generally in recent years.[4] The health sciences students were least likely to have used drugs (1.3 per cent). However there were differences between the health sciences students: the physiotherapy students had on average a higher consumption than the nursing and medical students. Figures two, three and four show rates of drug use in each of the three groups, differentiating between current and past drug use (last month, last year, and ever).

Further information emerged when we looked at the social and cultural characteristics of each group, and a

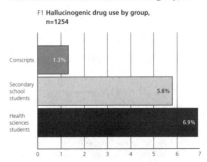

F1 Hallucinogenic drug use by group, n=1254

Fig 24   An example of a published research article
Source: Martinez Diez *et al.* (1999)

PAPERS
DRUG ADDICTION

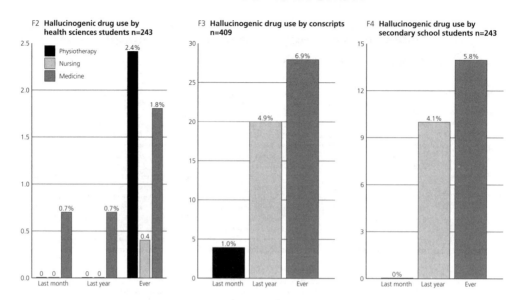

F2 Hallucinogenic drug use by health sciences students n=243

F3 Hallucinogenic drug use by conscripts n=409

F4 Hallucinogenic drug use by secondary school students n=243

number of significant variables became clear. Group one, the young people enrolled on the health sciences programme, were more highly educated, came from more affluent social and family backgrounds (middle class), and were more knowledgeable about the effects of drugs on health. They also had least problem with personal identity. The second group, the military conscripts, were a much more heterogeneous group, reflecting a broad cross section of economic, social and cultural backgrounds. Significant to this group was their total immersion in a social context of peers, away from their families and homes, and so exposed to greater peer pressure. The third group, the secondary school students, were of medium educational level, and generally from lower middle class family backgrounds. Their reasons for using drugs appeared to be linked primarily to experimentation, and peer pressure.

Discussion

From the analysis of social-cultural backgrounds, we were able to identify two important factors in the consumption of LSD: namely, exposure to peer pressure and lower educational, economic and social background. Taking these three groups as together representative of the population of young people in the principality of Asturias, it seems clear that strategies to tackle drug use should be focused on those identifiably at greater risk, measured by these two main characteristics. Strategies open to us, from those developed in Spain in recent years to combat drug use, operate at primary, secondary, and tertiary prevention levels.[6]

1 Primary prevention: aimed at young people who have never used drugs. The aim of such interventions is to stop first use of drugs and lessen the risk factors associated with first use. The main strategies at this level are health promotion through personal and social health education; reduction in availability of drugs, and reducing demand for drugs.

2 Secondary prevention: where primary prevention strategies have not been applied or have not been sufficiently developed, and drug use has started, although the individual is yet to become seriously addicted. The main objectives here are early identification and referral for treatment. This might involve individual or group surveys of the kind reported here, or individual clinical interviews with individuals thought to be at risk.

3 Tertiary prevention: when preventive measures have failed, and it is necessary to deal with the consequences of continued and regular drug use. The aim here is the treatment and rehabilitation of the drug dependant individual, in order to prevent further deterioration of health, and even death.

For us, carrying out this study has been a really rewarding experience. It has provided us with the hard data to support local initiatives to reduce drug consumption among young people in the area. Equally important, it has given us an opportunity to contact the young people of our town and discover what they think about drugs, as well as the incidence of drug use. □

1 Casado Glez C et al. Consumo de alucinogenos en una muestra de jovenes del Principado de Asturias. *Jornadas Nacionales de Socidrogalcohol. Alicante* 1997; 24.
2 Sole Puig J. Modelos animales de psicosis experimental con psicoestimulantes y cannabinoides. *Jornadas Nacionales de Socidrogalcohol* 1996; 23.
3 Herreros Rodriguez O. Calidad de vida y uso y abuso de drogas en estudiantes de ciencias de la salud de la Universidad de Oviedo. Oviedo: Tesina de Licenciatura, 1994.
4 Hinojal Fonseca R et al. El uso de drogas entre los adolescentes de Asturias (Espana). *Boletin de Estupefacientes* 1985; 37, 2-3: 49-54.
5 Lopez Rodriguez JL et al. Consumo de alcohol y busqueda de sensaciones en jovenes que realizan el servicio militar obligatorio. *Jornadas Nacionales de Socidrogalcohol* 1996; 23.
6 Bobes Garcia J. Salud mental. Madrid: Sintesis, 1994.

Fig 24   *continued*

References

Asch, S. E. (1951) Effect of group pressure on the modification and distortion of judgements. In: *Groups, Leadership and Men* (ed. H. Gruetzkow). Carnegie Press, Pittsburg, Pennsylvania.

Ball, S. J. (1981) *Beachside Comprehensive – a Case Study of Secondary Schooling*. Cambridge University Press, Cambridge.

Barker, E. (1984) *The Making of a Moonie*. Blackwell, Oxford.

Brown, C. and Gay, P. (1985) *Racial Discrimination 17 Years After the Act*. Policy Studies Institute, London.

Kumar, R. (1996) *Research Methodology*. Sage Publications, London.

Langley, P. (1993) *Managing Sociology Coursework*. Connect Publications, Lewes.

Mack, J. and Lansley, S. (1985) *Poor Britain*. George Allen and Unwin, London.

Martinez Diez, N., Lopez Rodriguez, L., Casado, C. and Gonzalez Delgado, S. (1999) Hallucinogenic drug use among young people in Spain: a comparative study. *Mental Health Care*, **21**(10), 346–347.

Mayo, E. (1933) *The Human Problems of an Industrial Civilisation*. Macmillan, New York.

McNeill, P. (1990) *Research Methods*. Routledge, London.

Milgram, S. (1963) Behavioural study of obedience. *Journal of Abnormal and Social Psychology*, **67**, 391–398.

Rosenthal, R. and Jacobsen, L. (1968) *Pygmalion in the Classroom*. Holt, Reinhart and Winston, New York.

Sissons, M. (1970) *The Psychology of Social Class*. Open University Press, Milton Keynes.

Townsend, P., Corrigan, P. and Kowarzik, U. (1987) *Poverty and Labour in London*. The Low Pay Unit, London.

Index

Page numbers in *italics* refer to figures and tables.